PATSY ROWE

PUBLIC SPEAKING

NEW HOLLAND

First published in Australia in 2005 by
New Holland Publishers (Australia) Pty Ltd
Sydney • Auckland • London • Cape Town

14 Aquatic Drive Frenchs Forest NSW 2086 Australia
218 Lake Road Northcote Auckland New Zealand
86 Edgware Road London W2 2EA United Kingdom
80 McKenzie Street Cape Town 8001 South Africa

National Library of Australia Cataloguing-in-Publication Data:

Rowe, Patsy.
Public speaking.

ISBN 1 74110 189 1.

1. Public speaking. I. Title.

808.51

Publisher: Fiona Schultz
Editor: Monica Berton
Designer: Karl Roper
Printed in Australia by Griffin Press, Adelaide

10 9 8 7 6 5 4 3 2 1

PUBLIC
SPEAKING

Foreword

This is an important book!

We live in rapidly-changing times and the best way to survive, nay even thrive and flourish, is to become a 'life-long learning machine'. I encourage every one I meet to continue their learning, and I believe that education will be one of the boom industries of the twenty-first century.

Not only do we need to keep learning by attending educational events, but I have also found that teaching and educating others is the best way to learn anything. Becoming a proficient, confident and interesting public speaker will help you to educate others and to speed up your own learning process. That's why this book is important, because it can assist you in developing some critical skills that will help you thrive in your life, regardless of where your passion may take you.

The fear of public speaking immobilises many people. I have personally coached senior executives in major companies who are terrified of standing up in public and opening their mouths! It's amazing that such objectively successful business leaders can have this difficulty. This reinforces the reasons why Patsy Rowe chose to write this book. Reducing this fear, which from all available research suggests is endemic, can be achieved, and it is useful and educational books like this that make it reasonably easy.

Why are so many people afraid of public speaking?

Just imagine a class of four-year-old children in kindergarten, where the teacher announces that the Prime Minister will be visiting and a volunteer amongst the children is needed to make a speech of welcome. How many children would put up their hands immediately? Virtually all of them! Children do not fear public speaking, yet as adults, we have adopted this new habit of fear. Patsy's book will help you remove this unhelpful habit, and set you free to enjoy the benefits of confidently speaking in front of any audience.

I have been a full-time professional speaker for over eleven years, and it is a huge pleasure to face the ongoing challenges of educating various audiences with varying needs. I have learned much about human nature that has increased my ability to strategically influence others. That's another benefit you will gain from reading this book and implementing its ideas and strategies.

Patsy Rowe has a wealth of experience that she shares simply, effectively and practically. I congratulate her on sharing her wisdom and thank her for helping to increase the number and quality of educators.

Charles B Kovess LLB (Hons), LLM, CSP, MAICD, MAITD
Australia's Passion Provocateur
National President, National Speakers' Association
of Australia 2004–2005

Contents

Introduction

The ability to speak in public, to say something interesting and entertaining—and ultimately to be able to 'say a few words at the drop of a hat', is not nearly as hard as most people think it is. Like playing the piano, or learning a language, anyone *can* do it—it's just that some can do it better than others!

The time and effort you devote to planning, preparing and practising a speech will make a difference to your success and how quickly you achieve it. And with success comes confidence and the courage not only to speak more, but to really enjoy it!

Chapter 1
What Makes a Good Speaker?

All the great speakers were bad speakers at first.
Ralph Waldo Emerson (1803–1882)

This book can be used by anyone who would like to say a few words at a wedding or present a one-off speech. It can be equally useful to someone already on the speaking circuit who would like to go from 'free to fee'.

Your goal as a public speaker is to engage your audience physically, intellectually and emotionally. These attributes are developed in three ways:

- how you look, move and sound (your commanding stage presence—the physical impact)
- how well you have structured and packaged the material you are presenting (how you engage your audience intellectually with what you're saying—the intellectual impact), and
- how effectively and convincingly you present the material (how you say it—the emotional impact).

A good speaker is someone who looks the part, is well groomed and appropriately dressed, appears healthy and relaxed, makes good eye contact, has a pleasant vocal timbre and clear diction, is animated and articulate, matches the content of their presentation to the listeners' needs, and delivers their message confidently in language that an audience understands. A good speaker always knows *how* to deliver a good speech and recognises the two stages in planning one: preparation—researching and writing your speech; and communication—ensuring an effective delivery of your speech.

Above all, a good speaker must be confident. Once you've mastered this and feel capable of presenting yourself in a professional and authoritative manner, the next stage is understanding your material and communicating it in such a way that you establish a rapport with your audience. You need to be able to persuade your listeners to understand you, to believe you, and to pick up on the enthusiasm and excitement you have for your topic. They may not necessarily agree with your point of view, but they need to be impressed by what you've said and the facts and figures that you've given, or the arguments you've used to support your case.

How to Be a Confident Speaker

Feeling nervous and apprehensive sometimes starts days before you actually present. You may experience pain in your chest, wake up in a cold sweat, suffer from diarrhoea or nausea, have heart palpitations and be consumed by a general feeling of dread. You may wish to feign illness, leave the country or apologise that you've double-booked—anything to avoid having to 'stand up and speak'. You may promise yourself you will *never* agree to do this again. On top of these feelings of near-panic, you may suffer on the day itself with a dry mouth, sweating palms and a general feeling of shakiness.

The very idea of standing exposed and vulnerable in front of a crowd, going blank, being looked at, being listened to, being boring, being asked questions you don't have the answers to, and being criticised, contradicted or poked fun at, can be enough to bring on any feelings of fear. You may feel concerned because you've failed before, lost your place (or your voice!), or you've been heckled by an audience. The very thought of these experiences will set off your nerves again.

What Can You Do to Overcome Nerves?

It's natural to feel a degree of nervousness before you speak—many experienced speakers confess to this. However, thorough *planning*, *preparation*, *practice* and *performance* will go a long way to overcoming nerves. To avoid feeling nervous, make sure you've researched your material carefully, so that your facts are correct. Ensure that you've written your speech in a form that's easy to follow (such as on palm cards) and practise in front of a mirror and with a tape recorder. Next perform the speech on your own, without notes, so that on the day nothing will be new to you.

Rather than dwelling on how inadequate and apprehensive you feel and how you wish you'd never agreed to present this speech, think positive thoughts about how well prepared you are and how your audience will find what you have to say interesting. Don't talk yourself into being 'hopeless'—avoid internal monologues where you berate yourself for feeling the way you do. The *perception* of failure is as real as failure itself. Instead, visualise positive images. Recall times in your life when you've been successful and felt confident because you knew how to do something. Capture that feeling and hold on to it. Take it with you up to the lectern. Apply that experience of success and 'getting it right' to this moment. Remember, only you will know if you miss a line, a quote or a statistic. Don't let any glitches throw you—move on. There is no better antidote to nerves than experience—with every speech that you make you'll be more polished and more comfortable. If it's possible to present to charities, service organisations or sports clubs where no fee is charged, then do so. You cannot underestimate the value of practice. If you still suffer from nerves, try the following:

- Get to the venue with plenty of time to spare so you can check your appearance, meet the organisers, see where you'll be speaking, check the microphone, and generally feel more comfortable with your environment. Have a drink by all means, but don't drink too much. A sober speaker is always a better speaker.

- Whenever you think about presenting, establish the right perspective. Picture yourself in front of the audience speaking, smiling, moving confidently around the stage—holding them in the palm of your hand. This is how you want to present and this is the picture you need to keep with you at all times.

- Play a meditation or relaxation tape beforehand, perhaps in the car, and do some deep breathing exercises.

- Take three short breaths before you start and begin speaking on the end of the third exhalation. This will take your voice down a little so that it is at the right pitch.

- Smile at the audience before you begin speaking—this will not only relax you, but warm the audience towards you and create a receptive mood. Remember it takes 17 muscles to smile and 45 to frown—so smile!

- If your legs feel weak and your knees shake then stand with your weight evenly distributed on both feet and rest one hand on the lectern for support. This feeling will disappear once you get going. If you stand behind the lectern, you'll feel more 'protected' in the knowledge that no one can see you're shaking.

- If you're a novice speaker, holding your papers or palm cards can be helpful because it gives your hands something to do. But if your hands shake during public speaking, put the papers or palm cards on the lectern.

- Try to imagine that the audience is made up of friends and family who all like you and want you to do well—they're on your team! The audience *wants* you to succeed, they *want* you to be interesting, and they *want* to go away informed, inspired or entertained. With all this positive energy in the air to help you to succeed, you will feel you're in friendly territory and this, in itself, will take away much of the anxiety.

- Allow your enthusiasm for your topic to show through, because the more passionate you are about what you have to say, the more you'll 'forget yourself' and speak naturally.

- Focus on three or four friendly faces scattered in the crowd and speak to them as if you know them personally.

- Make sure that you use a coloured highlighter on your papers or palm cards to distinguish the topic sentence—the main sentence of each paragraph—so that if you lose your place you can glance at the sheet and pick up where you are easily. Another technique is to use headings in the margin. For instance, if the paragraph is about a new medication for asthma, then you might print in red 'Flexitide'. Seeing the name will remind you of what you were going to talk about and you're off and running again.

- If you lose your place—don't panic! Look at the margin heading and either ad lib or take a sip of water until you find your place. Chances are that no one will notice if you miss something, because only you knew what you were going to say anyway. Take a deep breath and start again. Remember, there are very few occasions when an audience is 'hostile'; most people will admire you for speaking at all, so try to remember this and do your best. It will get easier every time!

- If your mouth tends to dry out when you get nervous, put a tiny piece of lemon in each corner—this will keep the saliva flowing. Otherwise there are excellent saliva substitutes available from most pharmacies, such as Aquae (a spray) and Oralbalance (a gel), which will alleviate a 'dry mouth'. Having a glass of water nearby is also a good idea in case you cough. Avoid drinking iced or chilled water, which can constrict your throat.

- If the overhead projector doesn't work, don't fiddle. Forget it and go on without it. In fact, don't fiddle with anything.

TAKE YOUR AUDIENCE ON THE JOURNEY WITH YOU

Another sure-fire way to improve your confidence is to learn how to take the audience through the speech with you. Your presentation must be logical, clear, unambiguous, and able to engage the audience with your enthusiasm and passion. To do this you need to tap into their feelings. About 90 per cent of our decisions in life are based on our feelings, and an audience will decide with their emotions whether or not they'll go on that journey with you. Once you've won their emotional attachment and included them on your journey, their intellectual acceptance will follow. For example, a presentation on a dry topic, such as tax reform, will be more successful if you can access the emotions of the audience. All you need to do is avoid presentations that rely too heavily on fact and figure and ensure that at some point you 'press some buttons' in your audience and have them sit bolt upright in their chairs as you strike a chord with each and every one of them.

One way to do this is to make sure that the examples you use in your speech are relevant to as many members of the audience as possible. Go into their territory and touch them with personal and emotional analogies, and examples and anecdotes they can relate to. For instance, if you were speaking to a group of mothers it would be relevant to talk about educational opportunities for children today. They will identify with this and your speech will affect them directly. What you're saying now has relevance for them.

Make sure your personal stories, anecdotes or jokes are current or that the audience will definitely know what you're referring to; for example, Pearl Harbor or Hiroshima may not mean anything to a younger audience.

Questions or No Questions?

Whether or not you invite questions from the audience is up to you, but it's best to take questions once you feel you are a confident speaker. Taking audience questions depends on whether you want to answer them, how well you know your topic, and the amount of time available. If you've been asked to speak for 40 minutes and to allow 10 minutes for questions, then you have to do this. If you're prepared to take questions, it's a good idea before you begin to speak to inform your audience that you would prefer to answer questions at the end of your presentation, rather than throughout it. It's very hard to keep your train of thought on the rails if you're constantly being interrupted, and other members of the audience might lose track of the main thrust of your speech as you answer one question after the other. In addition, by continuing with your speech, it's quite possible that you'll answer the question anyway.

If a function is being run by a chairperson, the questions will usually go through them. Chairpersons monitor questions and eliminate the 'silly' or impertinent ones. If the questions are coming directly from the floor, and unless there is someone going around the room with a roving microphone, it's important that you repeat the question so that the rest of the audience can hear what it was, and then say, 'Could everyone hear that?' You may have to repeat it more clearly. Answering questions can be very useful because if one person hasn't understood part of your presentation, it's possible others might not have either. Answering questions also gives you the opportunity to 'flesh out' areas you only touched on earlier.

If you're asked a tricky question, this also gives you a little time to think. If you don't know the answer, just say, 'That's an interesting question. Unfortunately, I don't have an answer for it' or 'See me afterwards as I don't have an answer right now, but if you give me your details, I'll follow it up and get back to you'. If you're sincere about your expertise, it's important that you do follow this up. If you're not able to answer their question, you should still send an email to that effect, and try to suggest someone else who might have the answer for them. It doesn't take long, and it will further enhance your commitment to your subject and your willingness to help.

If you're asked a question for which you don't have the answer but you know someone in the audience who does, say 'Look, that's actually a bit out of my field but I know Bob Smith is here today. Bob, can you help us with this one?' Or you can ask 'Is there anyone here today who knows anything about...?' Once they have finished answering the question, seize back the floor, as you don't want to lose the momentum of your presentation.

If the audience has been drinking alcohol during your speech, it's probably a good idea to skip question time. Similarly, if there have been several speakers before you on the program, and there are more to come, or it's the end of the day (and the audience is anxious to have a drink), I'd also give question time a miss. Anyone who is really keen can ask you their question over drinks or send you an email. End on a high note and get off the stage.

How to Deal with Hecklers

If you're speaking at a dinner and copious amounts of alcohol have been consumed, you may find that some members of the audience become disruptive or cantankerous. If you suspect this might be the case, try to identify the ringleader and focus your attention on them when you start to speak. If they still heckle you, it's probably best to pretend you didn't hear them—the first time. If, however, they persist and the audience laughs, then laugh with them and move on. If you're lucky enough to think of a quick response, use it—but be careful it doesn't develop into a slanging match. If they continue to interrupt you, avoid losing your temper and remain unflustered and smile, because the aim of the heckler is to unsettle you. A lot will depend on what they say, but if you can turn the spotlight on them with a witty comment which belittles them in some way, the audience will then be laughing at them, and with you.

If all else fails, it may be necessary to indicate to the organisers that you would like that person removed. Keep talking and ignore any scene taking place in the audience, who will feel for you, and in that way the episode can be turned to your advantage.

Chapter 2

Researching and Writing your Speech

To steal ideas from one person is plagiarism, to steal ideas from many is research.

Anon

You need to plan, prepare and practise your speech before you actually present it. Researching the topic of your speech is part of the planning process and involves analysing your potential audience and understanding your topic thoroughly. Before you begin to research and write your speech, you must know why you're speaking and to whom. It's crucial that you ask the organisers:

- Why did they choose you to speak today? Who spoke for them last year? What was the feedback on that person?
- What is the history and background of the organisation? Does it have strong political affiliations? What are its aims and objectives? Who are its patrons, if any?
- Will there be other speakers on the agenda? If so, who are they, and how many?
- Who will your audience be? People you know? People you don't know? People who know who you are?
- Will any VIPs or senior executives be present and, if so, what are their full titles and names so you can address them at the beginning of your speech?
- What are the demographics of the people who will be listening to you—their age, their education, their position, their social background and their sex? It won't always be possible to know a great deal about the composition of your audience,

but ask the organisers as many questions as you can before-hand. If you want to 'hit the spot' with your audience, you need to tailor your message to them. The more the audience perceives you as being 'as one' with them, the more open they'll be to your ideas and your point of view, so spend some time establishing who they are so you can target them.

- How many people will be in the audience?
- Will they have specific knowledge to enable them to understand industry jargon?
- Why are you speaking? To explain? Inform? Persuade? Convince? Entertain? What are their expectations?
- To what extent has your talk been promoted—internally within the company, externally in the media, or both?
- Will any media be present?
- Have other speakers spoken to the audience on the same or similar topic?

It's necessary to know the answers to these questions so you can present your speech effectively.

THE IMPORTANCE OF RESEARCH

The next step is to research your topic thoroughly. You need to know everything you possibly can about your subject matter to deliver it with confidence and to be able to answer questions asked by the audience. Even if you feel you know your topic well, extra research can be beneficial in either updating your material; supporting it with new statistics, figures and quotes; or injecting it with a little humour. Keep your eyes open for an anecdote or a few wise words from someone in the same field to add interest to your presentation. You may want to use visual support such as slides, videos or graphs to illustrate your content.

When you feel you have collected as much information as you need, write down the topic you are speaking about and, keeping it in front of you, start to evaluate what material you can use and what can be kept for a future presentation. Every time you make a decision to use something, look at the topic and make sure that what you intend to use is pertinent.

Confine yourself to making a few points so listeners will remember them, rather than trying to cover too much information and confusing them. A few points supported by anecdotes, examples and/or illustrations, given in an entertaining style, will prove effective. If you feel unable to cover as much as you would like in the allocated time, perhaps a handout with more details, statistics and graphs can be given out to attendees.

> When using statistics, try to connect them to something, so your audience can visualise. For example, rather than saying 33 per cent of the population has tried hard drugs, try saying, 'Look at the person to your left. Look at the person to your right. Statistically, at least one of the three of you has experimented with hard drugs ...'

STRUCTURING YOUR SPEECH

Defining the structure of your speech is part of the preparation process and occurs once you've assembled all the data from your research. Your speech should have three parts: an introduction, a body and a conclusion. For example, a 30-minute presentation would have a three-minute introduction, 24-minute body and a three-minute the conclusion.

A general guideline is to allow 150 words per minute as your speaking time. So, for example, if you've been asked to speak for 30 minutes, you'll need to write 4500 words in total (150 words by 30 minutes) to meet your allotted speaking time. This is approximate and, remember, if you tend to speak quickly, it's wise to slow down so that you don't appear nervous, and so older people who may have hearing difficulties, or those in the back row, don't find your presentation hard to follow. Ideally, four, perhaps five main points, is all you should attempt to cover in this time, so allow three to four minutes to fully develop each point you're going to make.

Lastly, a speech of any kind must have unity, variety, clarity and relevance. These factors are the building blocks of a cohesive presentation and will help you create a logical and balanced speech.

UNITY

Unity means that the flow of your speech is solid—it 'holds together'. There are four ways to achieve this:

1. Use examples to illustrate your point.
2. Use anecdotes that support your argument or point.
3. Use explanations to expand your main ideas.
4. Use comparisons to show the advantages of a line of action and then focus on what disadvantages might arise from that.

Every paragraph of your written speech should flow on to the next. For instance, if your last sentence stated that 'sales were down', your next paragraph could begin with the same words and explain why sales were down. Linking paragraphs maintains the unity of the speech.

VARIETY

To ensure that your speech is lively, use a wide level of word usage and vary your sentence lengths, so that you intersperse your medium to long sentences with short ones. This lends emphasis and is useful when you want to capture your audience's attention for a particular point you have made, for example, 'sales are more than down, sales are dying'.

Vary the way in which you begin your sentences, remembering to put the most important point at the beginning of the sentence. For example:

- *Crowds* (noun) began to gather …
- *Disgusted* (participle) by what I'd just seen …
- *Silently* (adverb) I watched in horror as …

Avoid beginning sentences with the same word, (unless you're using repetition to enforce a point.) Use a thesaurus for appropriate synonyms (words with a similar meaning) and antonyms (words with an opposite meaning) and make sure you're using the best word to achieve maximum impact.

CLARITY

Simplicity is the key to an effective speech, so don't clutter it with abstract terms, jargon or long-winded sentences.

RELEVANCE

When you start to prepare your speech, you need to ask yourself, 'What am I trying to say?' and 'What is my theme?' These questions will help you stay focused on what is relevant in your speech.

For example, if you're talking about crime increasing, take a piece of paper and brainstorm points that come into your head, pausing to refer to your research to check that your facts are correct. Don't worry about order at this stage; you're just letting the ideas come out as you have them.

When you feel you've written down as many points as you can think of, read them, shuffle them around, and arrange them into some sort of order—and only then number them. If you do this on the computer then you can cut and paste your points. Now, look at the points you've brainstormed and check whether they are relevant. Select only those that link in or support a coherent argument. If you find you're off the track, you need to be firm with yourself and sacrifice points which may interest you, but do not directly relate to the purpose of your speech. Cross them out and renumber the points you want to keep. This is the framework on which you will hang your information.

At this point it can be helpful to put your work aside, take a break, and return with a fresh mind. When you return to preparing your speech, refer to your points again and be very sure that everything relates to the topic you're going to talk about. If you have a very clear, well-developed structure, the audience will be able to move through the points with you as you present them. If you're using visuals you might like to list all your points and highlight the ones you intend to discuss in detail.

WRITING YOUR SPEECH

Once you have established the points you wish to discuss, write one paragraph to deal with each one. Assuming that you have 10 points, you will need to write 10 paragraphs of about 200 words each. It's too much to expect an audience to take in 10 points, however, and you might prefer to discuss four or five in detail and simply refer to the others, or discuss five in detail and give a handout on the other five. It has been shown that the more points a speaker attempts to make in a presentation, the fewer details the audience will remember.

The next step is to start writing your final speech. A good speech is broken into three parts: an introduction, a body and a conclusion.

Introduction

An introduction should capture your audience's attention, point them in the direction your speech will take them, and establish your credibility.

An audience recalls most information from the beginning and the end of a presentation, while the body of the speech is usually forgotten. You have about 30 seconds to capture an audience's attention and it is during these first 30 seconds that they will make up their minds about what they think of you and what you have to say. To make an impact, it's imperative that your introduction is as interesting, arresting and as punchy as possible. Try to outline or state the purpose of your presentation in one sentence that can be easily digested by your listeners. It's much easier to put the audience into a receptive mood if you open with:

- A quote—this can be from an expert on the subject you're speaking on, or it can be anonymous, as long as it's relevant to your speech. It should be short and you need to memorise it so you can deliver it with authority.
- An anecdote—this is the brief telling of an incident which should relate in some way to what you're about to say. For instance, if you were to talk to a group of owner/builders about the building industry and its problems, you might begin with a personal anecdote describing the problems which occurred when you were building your own home and which led you to dismiss the builder and become the site supervisor. This would give you some credibility with the audience as they would realise you've been a 'hands on' person in the industry.
- A question—a very effective technique to unlock the mind of the audience. For example, 'Why are so many young men committing suicide?'
- A joke (but be careful that it's both relevant and tasteful)—

if you can't think of anything original perhaps you can personalise a joke you have heard by adapting it so that you become the target and then you don't risk offending anyone in the audience. Re-jig a one-liner and mould it to suit your needs, your topic, or your particular situation.

- A thought-provoking statement or statistic—this is designed to get the audience sitting bolt upright within seconds of beginning your presentation. It would be something contentious such as, 'Abortion should be available to every woman who wants it'—but have facts and figures at the ready to support your argument.

Introductions should be brief and lead the audience into the body of your speech, so use this time to indicate what you're going to talk about. It's much easier for an audience to follow your speech if you've given some clues as to where you're taking them. You might want to show how your topic concerns them in some way, or you might begin with a rhetorical question or state an inflammatory comment that makes them sit up and take notice. You could quote some shocking statistics or facts on your topic, which would jolt them. To sum up, you need to:

- Spend time creating a powerful and memorable introduction which will acquaint your audience with you and your topic in two or three sentences.
- Be original, creative and daring—don't be afraid to shock; grab their attention with both hands and compel them to listen to you.
- Make sure that your introduction creates a springboard from where you'll launch into the body of your speech and the audience knows where you're taking them. Think of it as being a preview to the main event where you'll whet their appetite so that they sit expectantly looking forward to what is to follow.

Keep a file of press and magazine cuttings with witticisms, quotes, anecdotes and amusing incidents you can use when preparing a presentation. You can either quote the material as it is, or rework it to suit your needs. For example, I often use the following quote before my dining etiquette segment at my seminars:

The world was my oyster but I used the wrong fork.

Oscar Wilde

BODY OF THE SPEECH

Once you have the attention of your audience, move into the body of your speech, which tells the audience exactly why you're there. Begin each paragraph with a strong topic sentence, that is, the main sentence in that paragraph. As you flesh out that paragraph you are, in effect, building on that topic. Try to use examples to illustrate your point. Where possible keep your sentences short to medium in length, as this makes the sentences easier for your audience to take on board, and easier for you to say.

A topic sentence might be: 'There are three areas in which crime is increasing today.' Its brevity is forceful and we are immediately asking ourselves what those three areas are. In other words, the speaker has excited our imagination with a powerful statement. The rest of the paragraph should tell us what those three areas are and expand on them.

The next topic sentence might be: 'What can we do about this?' Note the use of 'we', which immediately draws the listener in and makes them feel invited to be a part of the solution. A rhetorical question is always guaranteed to inject curiosity into a speech and the body of this paragraph could outline the steps the speaker feels can be taken to solve the problem. So you can see that the speaker presents the problem and asks the listeners to think of a solution.

You should only use visual supports if you feel that your speech would benefit from them. Visuals should not be relied on to provide the main interest in your presentation. It should be your style, what you have to say, and the way you present your material that keeps your audience enthralled. Here are two techniques to use to link your points in a speech:

- **Arrows:** these are directionals for both you and your audience to follow. For instance, by stating that there are three reasons for increasing crime, you are reminding yourself where you are in your explanation, and you're also giving a sign to the audience that there are three reasons to be discussed.
- **Liaison:** linking one concept or idea to another can be done by using phrases such as, 'We can see that drugs play a part in the increasing crime, but let's look at what role they have to play in prison life itself.' This way you are reiterating a point you have just made and using it as a bridge to take you to the next point.

THE ROLE OF QUOTES

Quoting the words of other experts can be beneficial in that it lends an air of authority and credibility to your own assertions. When you use quotes from experts, make sure they *are* from an expert. Establish their bona fides and their credentials—what university did they attend or what paper did that quote come from? Use quotes and data from reputable experts and educational establishments, and always credit the source.

THE ROLE OF STATISTICS

Using an endless stream of statistics in any speech is guaranteed to send an audience to sleep. Statistics can be very useful if they are scattered throughout a presentation, but you must tie them in to the topic and give them a 'human face' so that they mean something to your audience.

Conclusion

Since your audience is more likely to remember your last words rather than your first, your conclusion should be as powerful as you can make it. It should also be brief, simple and sum up the main points you've covered in the body of your speech, bringing your audience back to the purpose of why you're speaking to them today.

Try to tie your concluding remarks to your opening remarks—you should not be introducing new points at this time but pulling the threads together. For a 20-minute speech, a minute should be enough for a closing, that is 150 to 200 words.

Ending with a quotation is always effective, reiterating the theme is important, and choose words or thoughts that you want the audience to leave the room with—a call to action ringing in their ears. This is your last chance to win them over, to send them away determined to live a different life, end a relationship, or look for a new career. Above all, your goal is to end on a high note so that they go away feeling moved, entertained, empowered, inspired—or all of the above!

Practice

Concert pianists, dancers, actors and athletes all practise for weeks and even years to prepare for their performance or competition. Speakers need to do the same. The more you practise, the more confident you'll feel when you present. Ideally, you should practise in front of someone (preferably not someone who loves you or works for you, as you might not get an unbiased opinion). I find it works to practise in front of a mirror. Other speakers have told me they find this impossible, but a mirror tells me if I am waving my arms around too much or moving awkwardly in a particular style of jacket.

As far as practising the content, you'll pick up words that are tricky to pronounce, long-winded sentences that leave you panting, and above all, you can time yourself. You'll be able to judge whether everything in your speech is relevant, whether your notes are easy to handle, and whether you'll be able to manage overheads or a PowerPoint presentation comfortably.

CHAPTER 3

ENSURING AN EFFECTIVE DELIVERY OF YOUR SPEECH

Say not always what you know, but always know what you say.
Claudius (10BC–54AD)

Every speaker develops their own style of delivery, the trick is to discover your hidden talents and use them. If you're a natural with accents, use them; if you're a born raconteur, tell stories; and if you're a humorist, tell jokes. Any of these talents can be incorporated into the four methods of speech delivery:

1. Memorise your speech. An actor may succeed in doing this and deliver their speech with passion and credibility, but most public speakers can't. If you try to memorise all of your speech, you run the risk of losing your place (mentally) and going into a spin. The best approach is to memorise the outline of your speech and tailor it to each occasion, but 'reciting' is unwise.

2. Read your speech. This is not as easy as it sounds. Unless you're a gifted writer and an expert reader with the ability to inject your speech with appropriate pauses, inflections and emphasis, it will be flat and colourless. If you *must* read your speech on the day, tape it as you would say it, then work backwards and type it up. Use that script as your speech so it will sound as natural and chatty as possible.

3. Impromptu speech. If you're known to be an interesting and lively speaker you may be asked to leap to your feet and 'say a few words'. If you speak frequently, you can grab a few 'slabs' of different presentations that suit the occasion; or

have a few witty proverbs, quotes or anecdotes at the ready and weave a few remarks around them. In any case, ask yourself: 'Why have they asked me to speak?' (your purpose), and begin by answering that question: 'I'm delighted to be asked to farewell our colleague, Tom Smith …', then work in a couple of anecdotes about Tom's career and conclude your speech.

4. The extemporaneous speech. This is by far the best way to deliver a speech. You write your notes and read them (and practise them out loud at home) so that you're very comfortable with the material—so comfortable that you will memorise your clever opening and conclusion and the *links* which take you from point to point. The rest will slot in and you can say something 'off the cuff' if you like and you have the freedom to 'move around' within the speech.

THE ROLE OF HUMOUR

An effective way of relaxing an audience and establishing a rapport with them is to make them laugh. In fact, it has been shown that the retention rate of an audience is considerably increased if there has been humour in the presentation. If an audience enjoys your speech, if they have some fun with you and a few good laughs, it will be much easier to persuade them to your point of view.

There are many websites devoted to the quip, the witticism, the clever opening line, to irony and the understatement. Humour should always be in good taste, so adapt any jokes to fit your particular topic. Think of using a joke that relates to your particular audience. For example, if you're speaking to a conference of marriage celebrants you might select something that concerns them. A quote that I like is from Marie Corelli, who said: 'I never married because I have three pets at home that answer the same purpose as a husband. I have a dog that growls every morning, a parrot that swears all afternoon, and a cat that comes home late at night.' You could add, 'Thank goodness for the future of our industry there are not too many around who think like Marie ... ' etcetera. It's essential that the joke, amusing anecdote or quote is relevant.

It's important to use humour wisely. Never use humour to target a member of your audience—you could end up looking callous and lose credibility. Avoid cluttering your speech with inane jokes—you don't want to lose the reason why you are speaking in the first place and turn your speech into a comic routine. Remember, the funniest stories can come from personal experiences and normal everyday situations.

STYLE

This is *how* you speak—and the best speakers speak naturally, use short words that everyone knows, and short sentences that are easily understood. When you're writing your speech, write it as you would say it, using contractions (isn't, wouldn't), and colloquial expressions ('he kept *his eyes peeled* for interesting quotes to use in his speech') that you would use in everyday speech.

The trick to presenting a lively and entertaining speech is to use well-crafted words and good grammar to clearly convey the message you want to send to the audience. It's important that you spend time finding the right combination of words to use so that your speech has a greater impact.

THE FIRST PERSON

The first person is 'I' for the singular, that is, one person, and the plural is 'we' for more than one person. The second person is 'you' for both the singular and the plural. The third person is 'he', 'she' or 'it' for the singular, and 'they' is the plural for more than one person.

When you're talking, you'll speak in the first person, referring to yourself as 'I' so you'll need to be aware that in a long speech this could grate on the listener. If something you're describing is a team effort then, of course, use 'we' and give credit to those colleagues who worked with you.

ACTIVE AND PASSIVE VOICE

Active means that the subject of the verb (the 'doing' word), is performing the action and is therefore a more powerful form of expression. For example, 'I attacked the thief' has more punch than the passive voice: 'The thief was attacked by me.'

PAINT WORD PICTURES FOR YOUR AUDIENCE

Words have two kinds of meaning:

- **Denotative:** the meaning of the word as it appears in the dictionary; its concrete literal meaning, and
- **Connotative:** the figurative meaning which often involves using imagery (word pictures). Connotative meanings add richness and emotional impact to a speech because they often appeal to the senses and ignite our imagination. As you're describing a scene to your audience, help them to 'see' it and become a part of the picture. You can do this by employing the following methods:

    Visual imagery: using words to help the audience draw their own picture in their mind. For example, you might use a simile to capture the indolence of a lazy road worker by comparing him to Coleridge's 'painted ship': He was as 'idle as a painted ship upon a painted ocean', for what could be more 'idle', less active, than a 'painted ship'?

Auditory imagery: using onomatopoeia (a word imitating the sound associated with an action). For example, the 'crunch' of shoes on a gravel drive, the 'swish' of a silk skirt or the 'hiss' of a snake.

Tactile imagery: using words that match what we can 'touch'. What could be softer than the metaphor 'blue velvet of the night' or the 'sharp sting of the nettle'.

Olfactory imagery: using words that describe what we can 'smell'. For example, the 'stench of death'.

Gustatory imagery: using words that describe what we can 'taste'. For example, 'the salty fish flavour clung to my tongue'.

Your goal in speaking to an audience is to communicate with them in clear language they will understand. By using imagery you will give your speech light and shade; you'll bring it to life and increase the emotional temperature of your audience. Below is a list of devices that help to create imagery, which will lift your speech and make it memorable:

- **Alliteration:** repetition of an initial sound, for example, 'terrible twos', 'swinging sixties'.
- **Repetition:** When a word or phrase is repeated to make a point, for example, 'I felt so alone, more alone than I'd ever felt in my life'.
- **Metaphor:** using a figure of speech to describe an object or action, for example, 'He is a wolf in sheep's clothing'.
- **Simile:** When two things are compared using 'like' or 'as', for example, 'Her eyes were as blue as the sky'.
- **Hyperbole:** using exaggeration to emphasise a point: for example, 'I could sleep for a week'.

- **Personification:** giving a personal attribute or character to an object to make it more interesting, for example, 'The table groaned under the weight of the feast'.

STYLE PITFALLS

Just as the way you dress reflects your personality, so does the way you present. Be yourself. Don't try to impress your audience by using big words, jargon or fancy phrases—your knowledge of the topic will impress them. Your aim is to communicate with your audience—if they have trouble following you, you're not communicating!

GRANDILOQUENCE

Avoid grandiloquence, which is writing that is highly embellished with over-inflated phrases or unusual words. Good writing is fluent writing—you don't have to 'dress up' your writing by using big words. Often, when writers try to impress by using grandiloquence, they use words incorrectly or in the wrong context. Unnecessary large words will not impress your audience; they're more likely to perplex them and to confuse the message you're trying to convey. For instance, the previous paragraph can be grandiloquently rewritten as follows:

> Constructing sentences superfluous in vocabulary by way of oversized, ambiguous and perplexing words is not conducive to perspicuousness; it will not inspire your audience, but rather confound them and obfuscate the intention of the sentence.

The secret to good English is simple: use plain English. Talk to your reader on paper in the same way you would talk to them if they were in front of you. A more contemporary style of business writing now allows you to use colloquial English, which means that you can use contractions such as 'don't', 'can't' and 'they're'. You may also address people personally by using 'you'; identify with others by using 'we' (rather than the old-fashioned 'one'); and even in some cases, if the meaning of the sentence isn't compromised, use 'them' rather than 'him' or 'her'. In certain instances you may even begin sentences with conjunctions like 'and' or 'but', which link that sentence to the previous one or contrast with it, improving the flow of your speech.

Using colloquial language doesn't mean that you can resort to slang or that it's acceptable to use poor grammar and structurally incorrect sentences. Be careful of using idioms (words or phrases which have a meaning other than the literal one). For example, 'it's raining cats and dogs' may confuse those in the audience whose first language is not English.

Clichés, Jargon and Buzz Words

Avoid using stale or overused expressions known as clichés. In fact, avoid clichés like the plague. Often people use clichés in place of more simple and original language. Some common clichés are:

- few and far between
- the powers that be
- the crux of the matter
- through thick and thin
- an uphill battle
- to lift one's game
- the bottom line
- cutting edge
- learning curve
- self-starter
- in the red.

You should try to avoid excessive use of jargon, because the audience may not understand what you're talking about. Buzz words should also be avoided. In most cases, the simplest word is the best word to use. Keep your audience in mind when you're writing your speech. While you don't want to appear boring or condescending by using unadorned language, you also don't want to pepper your speech with jargon or oversized words, which will leave members of your audience wondering what on earth you were talking about. Of course, if your audience is made up of university lecturers, then you can afford to use more sophisticated language. If not, it's best to use a mixture of words so as not to appear either oversimplistic or arrogant—keep the average person in mind; if you don't think they'll understand a word, don't use it. Some common buzz words and jargon to avoid are:

- 'address' to mean 'discuss'
- 'empower' to mean 'enable'
- 'parameter'
- 'paradigm'
- 'peer pressure'
- 'cool', 'groovy' or 'fab'
- 'impact on' to mean 'affect'
- 'utilise' rather than 'use'
- 'attain' rather than 'get'
- 'implement' rather than 'do'
- 'transition' rather than 'change'
- 'dialoguing' rather than 'speaking'

If you're concerned about excessive use of jargon, buzz words or clichés, you can edit the dictionary of your word processing program so that it marks clichés and other trite phrases as grammatically incorrect. You can then concentrate on rewording them when editing your speech.

Tautology

This common and frustrating error revolves around overstating issues by using two words with the same meaning or using extra words that fail to clarify the meaning in a sentence. For example:

- In *my opinion I think*.
- I've had to change my *mental thinking*.
- Please *return* that *back* to me.
- The *unemployed* who *haven't got a job*.
- Have you got the *exact facts*.
- *Everyone* has *unanimously agreed*.
- Let me *repeat* that *again*.
- There have been some *new innovations*.
- No company should have the *entire monopoly*.
- The *future prospects* of our clients are excellent.
- The *reason* why is *because*.
- We offer you *good honest* value for money.
- We have no *false illusions* about what you can or can't do.

Ornate or Pompous Phrases

Like grandiloquence, pomposity occurs when speakers use grand and dignified words to inflate the importance of what they're saying. The following sentences can all be made more effective by being simplified:

- I write to you today with a view of ascertaining your recommendations on …

  I am writing to you to find out what you would recommend …
- We shall acquaint you with the expected outcome.

  We will let you know the result.
- This move is expected to ameliorate the difficulties your company has experienced.

  This move should improve things for your company.

- Please confirm in writing, informing this office of the date at which these changes will be effected.

Please confirm in writing a date by which these changes will be made.

AMBIGUITY

Ambiguity is an error often brought about by poor sentence structure. A sentence becomes ambiguous when it has more than one meaning or has a meaning other than the one intended. As an example, 'Bring the client's file in any case', could mean bring the file in 'any bag or briefcase' or could mean 'regardless of what else you bring, make sure you bring the client's file'. Similarly, the sentence, 'Kathryn saw lions flying over Africa', could mean she saw flying lions, or that while she was flying over Africa she saw lions below. Both sentences should be rewritten as follows: 'In any case, ensure you bring the client's file', and 'While flying over Africa, Kathryn saw lions on the grassland below.'

VERBOSITY

Verbosity or wordiness occurs when unnecessary words, which are not crucial to the meaning of the sentence, are added. An example of verbosity is, 'an improvement in the volume of cheese production may be confidently anticipated in the event of an increase in herd numbers in the near future'. This sentence would be better written as 'cheese production will increase if we buy more stock'—which is exactly what the first sentence meant to say.

DISCRIMINATORY LANGUAGE

The advent of political correctness saw many common words denounced as sexist or discriminatory. As a result, in recent years, we have moved away from using words that are prejudicial against women, racial minorities or people with disabilities. Be conscious of this and use indeterminate words wherever possible, such as, 'police officer' instead of 'policeman' or 'policewoman', 'actor' rather than 'actress', and 'manager' rather than 'manageress'.

The use of the personal pronoun 'his' or 'her' can get very messy when used repeatedly. Where 'his' used to be the norm, it is now common to use 'their'. Often sentences can be rewritten to eliminate the problem of discriminatory pronoun use. For instance, rather than writing, 'The duty of a manager is to supervise his or her staff and to keep his or her administrative obligations under control', you could write, 'It is a manager's duty to uphold administrative obligations and to supervise staff'. A way of getting around an instruction such as, 'Every employee should park his or her car in the staff car park' would be to write, 'Employees should park their cars in the staff car park'.

It's also wise to avoid discriminatory language that includes unnecessary 'qualifying' information. For example, 'The vice president, a woman, will address the members', or, 'The man, who was in a wheelchair, went to the bank'. Do not stereotype. For example, don't write, 'The doctor put his bag in the car but the nurse put hers in her lap', unless in the specific example you're sure that the doctor is male and the nurse female. Don't always make CEOs, doctors, lawyers or politicians take the personal pronoun of 'he' or 'his'. Similarly, don't always assume that homemakers, hairdressers or beauty therapists should take a feminine pronoun.

WHO VERSUS WHOM

Often people are at a loss when it comes to deciding whether to use 'who' or 'whom'. 'Whom' is less frequently used nowadays, but it is still correct to use it in some instances. A good test to see whether to use 'who' or 'whom' is to think of who is doing the action and try to turn that sentence around to make the subject either 'he' or 'him'. Where 'he' would fit, use 'who'; where the answer would be 'him', use 'whom'. For example, in the question, 'To whom should I write the cheque?' the answer would be, 'Write it out to him", not, 'Write it out to he', therefore 'whom' is correct here. If you're ever unsure use 'who', to be on the safe side.

GRAMMATICAL TRAPS TO WATCH FOR

Although many points of grammar are frequently superseded or ignored in today's society, don't think that enunciation and grammar are no longer important—they are! The basic rules of grammar and word usage should still be observed. In any case, you won't be incorrect if you choose to ignore contemporary changes in favour of traditional grammar, although you may appear old-fashioned or pedantic. It's best to avoid some of the common grammatical errors listed below:

'Did' instead of 'done'	*'I did it last week.'* ***not**, 'I done it last week.'*
'Well' instead of 'good'	*'I did it well last week.'* ***not**, 'I did it good last week.'*
'Really' instead of 'real'	*'She is really tired.'* ***not**, 'She is real tired'.*
'As' instead of 'like'	*'She did it as I had done it.'* ***not**, 'She did it like I did it.'*
'Been' instead of 'went'	*'She's never been there.'* ***not**, 'She's never went there.'*
'Gone' instead of 'went'	*'I should have gone there.'* ***not**, 'I should have went there.'*

'From' instead of 'off'

'She took it from me.'
not, *'She took it off me.'*

'Who' instead of 'which'

'A girl who lives near me.'
not, *'A girl which lives near me.'*

'You' instead of 'yous'

'Are you all coming?'
not, *'Are yous all coming?'*

'Me' instead of 'myself'

'If it were up to me, I would do it.'
not, *'If it were up to myself, I would do it.'*

'Have' instead of 'of'

'I would have done it.'
not, *'I would of done it.'*

'Drunk' instead of 'drank'

'I shouldn't have drunk so much before coming on stage.'
not, *'I shouldn't have drank so much before coming on stage.'*

Chapter 4
How Do You Look?

Clothes and manners do not make the man; but when he is made, they greatly improve his appearance.

Henry Ward Beecher (1813–1887)

An audience judges you from the moment you step up on the stage. It only takes a mere 15 seconds for them to make that critical first impression. How you walk on to the stage, dress, and move about is very important if you want to create an impression that is commensurate with your topic. You want to convey the right image—a successful confident image—immediately.

How to Create a Good First Impression

All behaviour is communication of one kind or another. Your face, the way you use your eyes, your body, your posture, your gestures, your vocal pitch and your pace all combine to send out information to your audience about yourself, which they, in turn, unconsciously process. Your audience will decide whether or not they like you and want to listen to you in the first few minutes of your presentation.

You want to send an image of a fit, healthy, energetic person who is full of vitality and confidence. Regular exercise, good posture, a balanced diet, good grooming and well-fitting clothes are essential. It's difficult to convince your audience that you're a dynamic presenter if you clamber clumsily on to the podium, clutching your speech in one hand, perspiring and panting with the effort of climbing three stairs. Being overweight will also impede your breathing and someone wheezing into the microphone for the next 50 minutes will be both disconcerting and distracting. A speaker who removes his or her jacket to reveal a damp shirt or blouse will convey anxiety and tension.

Even though eating sensibly can be difficult if you travel frequently for your work, make the effort to exercise, so that your body is able to do the job you need it to do. A survey mentioned in the *Sunday Mail* indicated that 65 per cent of the people interviewed agreed that a woman's appearance is critical to her professional success—even more so than for a man.

What Should You Wear?

Firstly, decide on what style of clothing suits you best. For instance, a woman with heavy legs might look better in tailored pants rather than a skirt and low shoes might be more comfortable and easier to move around in than teetering precariously on high heels for 60 minutes. And shoes should always be clean, polished and in good repair because the audience often sees them at eye level when you are walking around the stage.

What colours are the most flattering on you? Do you look better in pastel shades or strong vibrant colours? Your clothes should reflect your personality and enforce your message. Think about how you want to be perceived—flamboyant, elegant, professional or conservative? If you're unsure of the way you dress, seek professional advice. An outsider will often identify a side of you that you haven't seen and advise you on updating your look.

Remember that you may need to wear a microphone with a box, so make sure that the tiny microphone can be clipped on to a blouse that opens down the front or a suit lapel and that the box can clip on to a skirt or pants. A one-piece high-necked dress would make this very difficult.

The audience may also be a factor in what you wear. For instance, if you were the last speaker on a Sunday at a convention and a barbecue was to be held right after your presentation (and your audience would therefore be wearing casual clothing), rather than changing when you finish, you might be more comfortable 'dressing down'. That isn't to say you would wear cut-off jeans, a merchandising T-shirt, or an off-the-shoulder peasant blouse, but be versatile and adapt your look: smart casual might create the right ambience for that closing presentation.

Avoid wearing any jewellery that dangles and jangles—swaying chandelier earrings can be distracting, as can charm bracelets rattling on wildly flaying arms. If you wear glasses, either take them off, or leave them on. Constantly removing them and replacing them is irritating and extremely distracting. Choose frames that complement your face shape and hairstyle or try contact lenses, especially if you feel your image is too 'bookish'. Neither men nor women should wear too much jewellery and rings through the nose, eyebrows or lips should be taken out. Make sure your handbag or briefcase is not bulging, worn or shabby.

THE BASICS OF GROOMING

You're trying to achieve a total look so your attention to grooming is just as important as your choice of clothes and accessories. Clothes should be clean, pressed, checked for hanging threads, lost buttons, sagging hems, scuffed shoes and laddered pantihose; and never stuff your shirt into your trousers. All these become a distraction for an audience looking at you and you alone.

For women:

• Hair should be clean, well cut with no unsightly regrowth.

- Make-up should be light—avoid glitter eye shadow or body shine
- Pantihose should not be fishnet, decorated or laddered.

For men

- Long hair should be clean and tied back.
- Moustaches or beards should be clean and trimmed.
- Hairy ankles should not be visible between the socks and the hem of the trousers.
- Shirts should be tucked in.

Body Language

Body language is a powerful tool to help you emphasise the important points in your speech. How you stand, smile, make eye contact and express yourself plays a huge role in how the audience will respond to you.

Posture

The most comfortable position (remember you could be standing for up to an hour) is with your feet apart so they're lined up under your shoulders with your weight balanced evenly between them. Avoid curling one ankle around the ankle of the other leg so you're balanced precariously on one leg.

Try not to slump over the lectern, grip it anxiously, or lean on it with both arms folded. Don't bounce from foot to foot, or adopt the Duke of Edinburgh posture, which is having your hands held together behind your back, and don't shove your hands in the pockets of trousers or jackets. Practise in front of a mirror until you find a position that is natural for you, which allows you to breathe comfortably and speak in a well-modulated voice.

Smile

Smile at the audience as you walk on to the stage, pause as you put your papers down, and then look at the audience again and smile. The warmth of your smile will not only warm the audience to you, but will transfer into your voice. Even if you're feeling tense and apprehensive, a smile will make you appear self-assured and in control.

Eye Contact

Use your eyes to make direct contact with members of the audience. Don't dart quickly from one person to the next; pause as you say a few sentences and direct them to individuals. Don't focus only on the front rows—start with them, then look to the back row, then to the right, and then across to the left and then back to the middle. Make everyone feel you're speaking to them; draw them in to what you're saying.

Be Expressive

The audience will be looking at you when you're speaking. Visual stimuli are important, so let both your face and your body help impart your message. Raise your eyebrows when you want to signify surprise, or if you want the audience to agree with you, ask them a question they can respond to, for example, 'I mean, do you think it's reasonable to hit me with that sort of a tax bill?' Invite them to ponder that remark with you. Perhaps tilt your head upwards to indicate a sense of hopelessness, shrug your shoulders, pull a face to signify disgust, or shake your head to convey, 'It doesn't make sense to me.' Your visual actions should underline your spoken message.

Hand Movements

Don't fidget with your hair, jewellery, tie or glasses. Avoid making short, staccato movements that can give the impression that you're nervous or ill-at-ease. Use wide arm movements that are sweeping and generous rather than short jerky ones. Movements support what you're saying, so match them to your words. For instance, if you were to say, 'I looked up at this *really* tall, handsome man', you might extend your right arm up above you to indicate just how very tall he was. At the same time, you might look upwards at your hand. The eyes of the audience will follow your hand and your eyes. They will be 'seeing' how tall this man was and re-living the experience with you.

The whole idea here is to 'act out' the scene you're painting with words, so you would emphasise the word *really*. Gestures are very important because they should harmonise with what you're saying, illustrate visually your verbal description, help you to describe the scene, and help the audience to imagine it. Practise at home in front of a mirror so that when you do it on stage, it's natural and appears spontaneous.

BAD HABITS

Video one of your presentations—or ask a colleague to critique you—to pick up the 'ums' and the 'ahs', the repetition of certain words or phrases, such as 'you know', 'you see' 'etc' or 'so on and so forth'. Clearing your throat, sipping constantly on a glass of water, yanking at your collar, stroking your tie, unbuttoning your jacket (only to re-button it seconds later), jangling your keys or loose change in your pocket, twisting a curl of your hair, adjusting an earring, and scratching your nose can become very distracting to the audience. Audiences are very susceptible to body language—watch yourself in front of a mirror and be aware of your mannerisms.

CHAPTER 5
HOW DO YOU SOUND?

Use what talent you possess: the woods would be very silent if no birds sang except those that sang best.

Henry Van Dyke (1852–1933)

When a speaker who has been trained in voice production (for example, an actor) delivers their speech, it has been estimated that about 85 per cent of the content is understood and retained, which drops to 45 per cent for the untrained speaker. This doesn't mean, however, that you need a voice coach, but you do need to listen to yourself and identify areas for improvement.

One of the main problems that many speakers have is delivering a speech that doesn't sound studied, stilted or forced. Try to speak as naturally as you can. To do this, it sometimes helps to focus on two or three faces in the audience and to speak to them directly, as though you were speaking to friends. Imagine you're telling them this story, explaining these statistics or trying to persuade them to your point of view. Using rhetorical questions can help in this regard. For instance, if you were to say, 'And what can we do about this situation? Well, there's plenty we can do. Everyone in this room today can do something!', this will help you to forget that you're speaking to an audience and you'll come across as more natural and spontaneous. There are two points we need to consider when we think of how we sound:

1. The pitch, tone and volume of your voice
2. Pause, pace and emphasis in your diction.

Your Voice

If you tend to have a high voice and being nervous exacerbates this, take three short breaths as you walk to the microphone, breathe out on the last step and start speaking at this point. Your voice will drop a little and you won't sound tense and tight. Increase the volume of your voice when you are stating something in earnest, and lower it to almost a whisper when you want the audience to 'lean in towards you' to catch a vital point you are about to impart. If you're relating something sad, let your voice reflect that. If you're relating something exciting; sound excited. Experience your speech; live it, don't just speak it. If you don't 'feel' sadness or relive the excitement of your story in your voice, how do you expect your audience to feel those emotions and respond to them? You're taking them on a journey of highs and lows, so let your volume and expression mirror this.

> Poor breathing is the culprit for most vocal problems, so breathe deeply before you start to speak, so your voice is being projected on a strong stream of air.

Pitch

You need a versatile range of pitch in your voice to sound interesting and 'alive'. If you're tense, your vocal chords will tighten and this will send the pitch of your voice up to an awkward, unattractive shrill. Getting the pitch right comes back to being relaxed and at ease. Avoid wearing tight collars, or a tight bra, or clothes around your upper body that impede your breathing.

Begin each new sentence by lifting your pitch a little, as it will drop naturally as the sentence continues. If you keep to the same pitch for the whole sentence, and the ones following, you'll sound flat and monotonous. Try taping yourself and listen carefully to whether your voice is 'moving around' as you speak. If you have ever been interviewed on radio, you would have seen in the studio a machine that follows the pitch and volume of your voice. Hopefully, it moved up and down like a heart beat.

The change of pitch on a stressed syllable is referred to as an inflection and we have level, downward or upward inflections. When we're speaking in a conversation, we stress some syllables of words—as well as complete words—more than others. Imagine a conversation you might have if you were fed up with your untidy daughter leaving a mess around the house. You might say, 'I am *so* fed up with cleaning up after you. This is the *last* time I do this …' Placing emphasis on certain words is what you need to do when you're speaking to an audience—it's a part of oral punctuation. This is what puts energy and sincerity into your speech and makes you sound as if you mean what you're saying.

Tone

This is what makes your voice unique. The tone of your voice is created in the 'hollows' of your body:

- your head lends a higher quality to your voice which is why a head cold will make you sound nasal
- your mouth shapes your vowels—even your teeth play a role as you need to speak from the front of your mouth, and if your teeth project, forcing your tongue into awkward positions, this may present a problem
- your chest contributes to the depth of your voice.

The best voice has a balance of these three areas working for it, so listen to your voice and get to know what it can do. Find your lightest and deepest tones and relax as you practise speaking so that your breath and your sound flow comfortably.

Volume

Being able to decrease or increase the volume of your voice adds colour and vibrancy to your speech—it's what makes it animated. Don't make the mistake of adopting a loud voice for your whole presentation in the belief that it makes you appear to be a more powerful speaker. Raising and lowering the volume of your voice is important to hold the attention of your audience—increase it when you want to provoke them, embolden them, and call them to action—and decrease it when you want them to sympathise or agree with you.

Your Diction

Good diction is the choice and use of the right words and their clear and distinct pronunciation. The very best way to know whether or not you're easy to understand is to tape yourself and listen to whether you are using a steady pace, emphasising key words, and pausing during your speech. If you feel some words are hard to say, change them for others. In fact, make a list of words that you note other speakers having difficulty with and avoid them. If your words 'get lost' through saying them too quickly, slurring them, or running them into the next word, practise them so this doesn't happen. You'll lose an audience very quickly if they can't understand you. Any words that may be unfamiliar to an audience need to have a slight pause before them and special care taken using them. Replace two- or three-syllable words with simpler ones. For instance, why say 'malevolence' when 'hate' is easier to hear and understand.

Keeping your lower jaw relaxed and mobile is important for clarity of pronunciation. Sometimes, if we're nervous, we tighten the jaw (or even grind our teeth) and so when we speak the words struggle to get out. Try yawning to free the jaw, or rub either side of the face near the ears with your second and third fingers to loosen it. We all carry nervous tension in different places but it's vital that the jaw be as relaxed as possible in order to achieve good diction.

Pace

Pace is the speed of delivery and often when we're nervous we tend to speak too quickly. If you tend to do this, you run the risk of the audience not being able to understand you, particularly if your diction isn't as clear as it could be. Record yourself on a tape recorder and be the judge. If you think you were too fast, slow down. This gives your audience time to take in what you're saying; to digest it. Slow down even more when you have something important to say and say it meaningfully. The trick is to vary your pace. When we're in a conversation with someone, we might speak very slowly to add meaning to what we're saying, for instance, 'I told her I would *not* do it.' This technique adds emphasis and importance to what you're saying. Do the same with a speech. Speak at normal speed, then slow down to indicate that something important is about to be shared with the audience, then say it slowly, with emphasis. You'll have their complete attention … and they'll remember the point.

Pause

Pausing is one of the most effective forms of vocal punctuation and gives your audience time to reflect on what you're saying— to absorb it. To do this you need to punctuate with pauses, not only with the volume of your voice, but with the suggestion of a smile.

For instance, if you're telling the audience of an incident that infuriated you, adopt an angry tone to underline this. Pausing in mid sentence *is* very effective. In other words, just before you say something important, give an astonishing statistic such as, 'There are seven young men who commit suicide in this country (pause) every day', or an amusing one, for instance, 'I think John was my second husband (pause) or was he my third?' (This would be accompanied by a feigned thoughtful expression as you tried to remember.) Pausing gives the audience a signal on what is to come and gives them time to *feel* the emotion you're evoking.

The pause is also very important with humour—not only just before you say something amusing to alert the audience to what is coming, but after you've said it to give them time to get the joke. Don't talk over their laughter; pause, look around and use a facial expression to underline what you've said. Above all, pause to let everyone relish the moment.

One of the most important places to pause is at the end of your presentation. Say your final words (which will be powerful and clearly your 'close'), and then pause and look at the audience. Let your last comment sink in. They will realise you've finished your speech and their response will be more dramatic than if you'd just collected your papers and said, 'Thank you'.

EMPHASIS

Emphasis is stressing a particular word or phrase in a sentence which can often completely change the meaning, for instance, '*He* wasn't the only one who did it' as opposed to 'He wasn't the *only* one who did it.'

Good speakers know the importance of vocal clarity. If your speech were to be *read* by the audience, you would need commas, dashes, exclamation and question marks to make the meaning clear. The spoken word depends on your voice, its volume, its light and shade and, most importantly, emphasis to punctuate your words.

The Microphone

Understanding the types of microphones available and how to use them is vital to speaking success. There are three types of microphones you need to be aware of:

- A stationary microphone. This is on a stand so your hands are free. Before you start speaking, adjust it to the correct height—usually up to your chin. The distance your mouth should be from the microphone is the length between your thumb and little finger when you spread out your hand. Position it correctly so that you're not leaning in awkwardly towards it with your head tilted to one side.
- A hand microphone (which can sometimes be removed from a stand). Make sure that you move it to the left, back to the centre, and then to the right as you move your head. You may want to change from one hand to the other, but don't swap it back and forth so that it becomes a distraction for the audience.
- A lapel microphone (with or without a cord). This type of microphone clips on to your jacket, blouse or dress and gives you the freedom to move around the stage or even walk out into the audience. If it has a cord, be wary of tripping on it if you turn quickly or walk backwards (and tape any loose cord with gaffer tape). Make sure you wear a jacket with generous strong pockets or a two-piece dress because the receiver 'box' of the microphone either clips on to the back of your trouser or skirt waistband or has to be carried in your pocket and some of the older ones are quite heavy.

It's important to test the audio system as soon as you possibly can after arriving. If there is a problem it might take time to rectify or require an expert to be called in.

Chapter 6

Visual Aids

If it keeps up, man will atrophy all his limbs but the push-button finger.

Frank Lloyd Wright (1867–1959)

Bear in mind that most people have limited attention spans, they tend to remember about one-quarter of what they hear and about three-quarters of what they see.

The primary role of visual aids is not to drive your presentation, but to help your audience 'see' the point you're trying to make. The second role of visual aids is to speed up the time it takes you to deliver your core message and communicate your ideas. And thirdly, a picture can often leave a stronger impression than a spoken word.

Visual aids can break up your presentation and help to hold an audience's attention. It's necessary to remember that visual aids are there not to compete with you as the presenter, but to *support* and *complement* what you say. Make sure that you don't disappear into a fog of frozen gas, throbbing music, sound effects or rapidly flashing slides. The audience is there to see you, and to hear you and your message, so avoid presenting a narrated slide show and keep your visual material simple, dramatic, brief and above all, in a supporting role to you—the star.

How to Use Visual Aids

Visual aids can give a professional touch to any presentation. When used skillfully, a combination of videos, slides, and music can be captivating, but you need to be technically competent, confident and well rehearsed. When using visuals:

- Familiarise yourself with the venue and make sure you know how to dim the lights and close the electronic blinds or curtains.
- Practise with the equipment at home before your presentation so you can avoid any unexpected and distracting equipment noises, which may break audience concentration.
- When you rehearse your speech, do so using your visual aids. Stand beside an overhead projector and, once you have made your point by referring to the screen, take your attention back to the audience and speak to them, not the image.
- Make sure that you 'keep pace', for example, if you're saying 'losses for this year' ensure that the screen isn't projecting 'profits for this year'.
- Use a laser pointer if you need to indicate points on a screen.
- When you refer to your support material, talk your audience through them and show them how they are linked to what you have just said.
- Turn visual or audio equipment on only when you are using it and turn it off once you have finished with it, so that neither a flashing screen or a whirring machine distracts your audience.

When creating visual aids, such as transparencies or notes, you need to consider how they will appear to the audience and whether they will be able to read them quickly and clearly. To ensure your visual aids look professional and well-designed:

- Make sure your text is legible and large enough for people in the back row or at the side to read it.
- Limit your theme colours to no more than three. Both blue and green are excellent background colours, with white or yellow text being very easy to read. A red background with

light contrasting text is spirited and forceful, while a black background conveys solidness and reliability. Choose your colours so that they match your message.

- Use lower case letters; only use capitals for titles, at the beginning of a sentence or for keywords.
- Use a sans serif font, which tends to be easier to read from a distance.
- Use the same font for the whole presentation.
- Use italics, underlining or bold for emphasis.
- Refrain from squeezing too much information onto one visual.
- Keep sentences short—three to six words per line is eye-catching.
- Place text in shapes so that it is 'contained', for instance, three circles on a page with a word in each circle will be more easily recalled than three words 'floating' on the screen.

When using visual aids you need to be aware of issues relating to copyright, libel and plagiarism. The source of material used in your printed notes and visual aids should be acknowledged—even photographs and information from the Internet can be subject to copyright. If you make sure that you give full credit when you use quotations, text, charts and photographs you don't always need to get permission from the publisher or author. The rules of copyright are complicated and sometimes you do have to pay for usage, in which case you may want to contact the author or publisher to make sure you are doing so legally.

Libel and slander is usually referred to as defamation and you are said to defame someone if what you say will expose that person to ridicule, contempt or cause them to be ostracised in some way by disparaging them in their profession or organisation. The distinction between the two is that something you write is libel and something that you say is slander.

Plagiarism refers to 'stealing' jokes, ideas or material from other speakers to pass off as your own. If you want to use other speaker's material acknowledge it correctly.

> Use visuals only when and where appropriate, but be prepared for glitches and carry extra bulbs, plugs, batteries, extension cords or anything else you might need.

TYPES OF VISUAL AIDS

Think of visual aids as being arrows directing your audience's attention to a point that you really want to drive home—the facts, graphs or statistics you may want to highlight. For example, if you're speaking for one hour, it would be appropriate to refer to a visual aid perhaps every six or seven minutes, giving you a maximum of say, seven or eight visual aids. When preparing visual aids, you need to consider the size of your audience, whether they will be standing or seated, whether they will need to take notes, and if they will be able to see the visuals clearly.

Audio and visual aids range from desktop presentation software and output devices, audio tapes, whiteboards, flip charts and videos to Internet link-ups. These tools provide flexibility and make it easier for the audience to absorb the material. There are many different types of visual aids to use; you just need to know which ones will most benefit your presentation.

PRINTED NOTES
Handouts or printed notes are best done on A4 sheets of paper that are stapled together. If time and the budget permit, you may want to present them in a folder or plastic sleeve, or bind and laminate them. Use a title page and request permission to include the client's logo to make the notes look as professional as you can. You can use

colour printing and remember to provide a slot in the back of the folder to hold your business card if you haven't included a page at the back of the notes with all your contact information.

Handouts are very useful as they eliminate the need for your audience to try to write endless notes, so they can concentrate on what you're saying. A good method is to write major points in a block down the centre of the page so that attendees can make notes in the wide margins on the left and right of your printed material, otherwise, include lined pages for personal notes. Number all the pages, use headings and subheadings, bold your keywords, use italics, and perhaps include copies of the graphs or charts you're showing.

Take the time to package your notes attractively—this will not only enhance an audience's perception of you as a speaker, but they are more inclined to keep them for later referral. So make sure that you include a page with your biography, website, titles of any books you have written and perhaps a page where attendees can order your books. Don't hand out these notes at the beginning of your presentation because attendees will start reading them, rattle the pages as you speak, and be distracted.

FLIP CHARTS

Flip charts are best used with smaller audiences of, say, up to 60 people. Keep your writing big and bold using a black texta pen, write or draw as you speak, and use colours to accentuate or differentiate your points and to make them more visually attractive.

Prepare your flip charts beforehand so that you're not using up valuable time writing and drawing when you could be indicating and elaborating. If, however, you want to generate some audience participation, then it's best to write on your flip charts during the presentation. Make sure your writing is legible so that the listeners at the back of the room can read it clearly. A disadvantage of using flip charts is that your back or side is facing the audience whenever you're writing. Another disadvantage can be the flipping back and forth of pages. If you're going to refer to previous pages in your flip charts, then tear them off and pin them up for the audience to look while you're speaking.

OVERHEAD PROJECTOR (OHP) AND TRANSPARENCIES

Overhead projectors (OHPs) and transparencies are probably the most popular visual aids of all because they are very easy to use, they don't require a dimming of the house lights, and they can be used with larger audiences because the images are projected onto a large screen. The guideline for an hour's presentation would be to use perhaps 10 or 12 visuals.

Transparencies have the advantage that if you have to condense your presentation at the last minute, because another speaker has run over time, it's very easy to drop transparencies out or change the order. Be careful not to construct your presentation on each transparency because it will then become tedious.

SLIDE PROJECTOR

Although more expensive than the OHP, slide projectors are easy to transport, organise, store and, above all, to use. In addition, they often give a better image, subtlety of colour and strong tones.

If slides are made into a format like PowerPoint, keep them simple without too much text and spend no more than a minute verbally elaborating on each one. Because they are operated by a hand-held remote control, the speaker is able to move away from the equipment and 'work' the stage.

A disadvantage to using a slide projector is that the room must be darkened for the screen to be seen. As the speaker, if you are too far away from the equipment and standing at the side of the stage in the shadows, you may become a faceless voice and the darkened room is conducive for the audience to slip into a somnambulant state. If, however, the audience is very large—in which case an I-Mag projection system can be used (usually on both sides of the stage)—this problem is alleviated.

OUTPUT DEVICES FOR COMPUTERS

Data projectors are relatively cheap and portable. Connecting a computer or laptop to a data projector (called an LCD projector [Liquid Crystal Display]) allows the content on your computer screen to be projected to a screen for the audience to view. An advantage of using this device is that the room lights do not have to be substantially dimmed to show strong colours and clear text.

POWERPOINT

Used with a data projector, Microsoft PowerPoint is a very flexible visual aid. It can be manipulated to include pictures, graphs, charts, text and sound while allowing you to customise the length each page displays on the screen. Once loaded, this program can run automatically throughout your presentation. You can also use it to generate printed notes.

IMAGE MAGNIFICATION TECHNOLOGY (I-MAG)

With I-Mag *you* are the visual, so the audience can see minute facial expressions and be more aware of your non-verbal messages. I-Mag screens are usually huge and therefore commanding. They have the advantage of being able to be seen from anywhere in the room and are excellent in that people at the back of the room enjoy the same intimacy as if they were sitting right in front of the speaker. Don't be distracted by the audience appearing to look behind you, or to the side of you, and speak to them without looking at the screens.

DIGITAL CAMERAS

Digital cameras can connect to a computer, allowing images to be shown directly on screen. Depending on the computer system, your photos can be displayed in a format similar to a Microsoft PowerPoint TM presentation.

VIDEO AND DVDs

If your video can be played on a large screen through the house system, it can be used for a large audience. If you're limited to a monitor the size of the average television screen, it will only be effective with an audience of say 50 to 80 people. It will be necessary to have a contingency plan in case of electronic glitches, as sometimes a tape can break or a DVD can be scratched.

QUESTIONNAIRES

If you feel it will benefit your presentation to have the audience fill in a questionnaire, draw a picture, or write down their goals on a piece of paper, try to avoid leaving the stage and distributing the material yourself. Arrange beforehand for someone to put these documents on the seats, and then to collect and assess them once the audience has completed them. If you break the rhythm of your presentation it can be difficult to re-establish it.

It's preferable to select only a few powerful aids than to be tempted to use too many. Too many visual aids will only tire your audience and detract from you as the speaker.

PROPS

Props to support a point you're making can be useful, but be careful that they complement your presentation, rather than detract from it. I watched a well-known presenter cut up a stuffed doll that she told us belonged to her seven-year-old daughter. The audience gasped as she cut off an arm, then a leg, and then the head. I can't recall the point of the amputations, only that I was so concerned as to what the child would say when she found out what her mother had done. Over drinks later, the general consensus was one of barely disguised dismay; many commented on the fact that it had been tasteless and, above all, no one could remember why she had done this, only that it seemed a very odd thing to do.

WHAT TO DO IN CASE OF AN EQUIPMENT GLITCH

If equipment starts to whirr, buzz or crackle so loudly that you can't talk over it and the audience is getting fidgety, suggest a 10-minute break, but remember this will halt the flow of your presentation and some of your audience may not return. Ask if someone in the audience is familiar with this sort of equipment and if they can help, or if someone can go and find the conference organiser or a member of staff who can perhaps advise you on how to fix the problem. If all else fails, turn off the equipment and fly solo.

CHAPTER 7

HOW TO GET
A GOOD INTRODUCTION

*Think like a wise man but communicate in the language of
the people.*

William Butler Yeats (1865–1939)

What the audience learns about you before you actually start speaking is very important because it can set the overall mood for your presentation. If you're to give a light-hearted, amusing presentation during a convention, your introduction would be very different from one used for a serious presentation.

When the booking for your talk is confirmed, find out who will be introducing you and post, fax or email the appropriate introduction to them. If possible, ring and chat with the introducer well ahead of the event and ask them if there was anything in the introduction that wasn't clear or that they might need help with. Be tactful; you don't want to offend them, but creating a rapport with them will help to achieve your goal of a good introduction. It will also help 'break the ice' and they will feel a little more at ease and therefore do a better job for you on the day.

If you aren't able to speak with them, you should still post, fax or email your introduction to them. Most people who are asked to introduce the speaker are not speakers themselves and frequently have little, if any, experience. So assume this is the sort of person who will be introducing you and plan accordingly. If you don't do this, you risk the introducer saying far too much about you and the audience is bored before you even go on stage, or they may crack one or two tasteless jokes that fall flat, which puts the audience in the wrong frame of mind. If they don't bother to do any research on you at all and try to 'wing it' you may be introduced so poorly that the audience is left wondering why you were invited there at all!

HOW TO WRITE YOUR OWN INTRODUCTION

When you begin to write your own introduction, it's important to outline what you want said about you and your subject area, taking care to highlight those aspects of your life or career that you feel will prepare an audience for what you have to say. For example, if your topic is on a serious subject such as 'How to save tax', your introduction would include the fact that you're a chartered accountant, you have written seven books on tax reform, and that you have been invited to speak at three overseas conferences on this subject. This gives you credibility and puts your audience in the right mindset to hear what you have to say.

It's important to take a copy of your introduction with you on the day of your presentation, because sometimes the person who has been selected to introduce you either falls ill and doesn't attend, they may have lost it, left it at home, or simply can't find it. Keep spare copies in your car, your handbag, briefcase, or speaking folder as they can also be handed out with your business card to anyone who is interested in having you as a speaker for their organisation.

Remember that a lot of people don't read well, so keep the language in your introduction simple, and use punctuation carefully so that it can be read *with meaning*. Many of those asked to introduce you are so nervous that they may stumble and stutter their way through it. That's why if you can email, fax or post your introduction prior to the event, they will have more chance to read it and be comfortable with what they have to say. This same introduction can be handed to the media if they attend on the day and to the producer or presenter who interviews you on radio. Bear in mind that everyone is very busy and has no time to do research so make it easy for them. If you have a website, you can post your introduction on it and suggest organisers print it off from there, but still take your own copies on the day.

Following are some great tips on how to write an effective introduction:

- Head it up 'Please read as written' to discourage improvisation.
- Write on A4 paper using 1.5 spacing, in either Arial or Times New Roman font, which are both easy to read.
- Use a 14-point typesize so people of all ages can read the text clearly.
- Use bold or italics for any words you wish to emphasise.

> To alleviate any possible offence taken by the introducer at being asked to 'Please read as written', I soften this on the day by explaining that it helps me enormously if they can do this for me as I have often found that if the introducer ad libs it can detract from my opening lines.

TYPES OF INTRODUCTIONS

Your introduction should always say something 'catchy' about you that will grab the audience's attention. It should also outline the reason why you were invited to speak and have some background information on you. Following are examples of a light-hearted and serious introduction.

Sample of
a Light-hearted Introduction

Start the introduction with something catchy:

> Patsy Rowe is the author of nine books, a professional speaker, columnist, critic, humorist and 'hanging judgette'. This was her nickname for six years when she sat in the role of a judge hearing cases against builders who overcharged or refused to complete a contract. Patsy was the only woman on a board of nine judges in New South Wales and lived to tell the tale, even if she did have to move to Queensland!

Next explain why you were invited to speak:

> Patsy's first book, *No Sweat Not to Worry, She'll Be Jake*—the story of building her own home before she was married (he was smart and proposed when it was all over)—went to the top of the best-seller list in record time. Patsy is the ideal person to talk to us today about how to renovate or restore our homes without lurching into a lifetime of debt, suffering a nervous breakdown—or both!

Now state some background information about you, the speaker:

> She began her career teaching Chaucer and Chekhov to novice priests at the Passionist Fathers Seminary, her second job was selling radial car tyres, and her last was as a national marketing manager selling microprocessors and semiconductors. If there doesn't seem to be any correlation between these jobs, that's because there isn't. Her proudest moment was winning first prize for her choko chutney; her proudest achievement was learning to set the VCR.

Finally, end with:

> I think we're all going to have a few giggles today hearing what Patsy has to say about how to handle those tempera-mental tradesman, so please welcome 'The Hanging Judgette' (pause here) ... Patsy Rowe.

SAMPLE OF A SERIOUS INTRODUCTION

Again, start with something catchy:

> It is said to be the rudest question you can ask: 'Why aren't you married?' Almost as bad in polite society is: 'I'm surprised you haven't any children yet.' Today Patsy Rowe is here to tell us how to keep our foot out of our mouths, or how to extricate it if it's already in there.

Next add the reason you were invited to speak:

> To get to the top of the business or professional world means gaining an extra edge over the competition. Easier said than done. We've invited Patsy Rowe here today to show us how to create that all-important first impression—the one you only get 30 seconds to make—and to guide us through the maze of today's gender etiquette.

Now state some background information about you, the speaker:

> Patsy has written three books on etiquette, has done over 380 talkback radio interviews in the last six months, appeared on national television, and writes a column entitled 'Do Manners Matter?' She gives lectures on business etiquette to corporations in Australia, New Zealand, the Far East and the USA, where she is in demand for her Boot Camp for

Blokes—a day of etiquette tailored especially for men. Who better to help us pick our way through the minefield of modern manners in this new millennium?

Then end with:

> She's here today to show us what to do, when to do it and, most importantly, how to do it, so please join with me to welcome (pause here) … Patsy Rowe.

As the speaker, you need to position yourself nearby so when the introduction is finished, you're on your feet and moving towards the stage. Shake hands with the introducer and thank them for their kind words. If a light-hearted introduction was used, you might like to say, 'Thanks Bob. I wish my husband was here today and could hear what an interesting person I am.' It's now up to you to lead in smoothly from the introduction so that by the time you're at the lectern, you're ready to smile at the audience and start your speech. You might even want to continue that comment to the audience: 'You know next time my husband complains about my cooking, I'm going to read him that introduction so he'll know what kind of a wonder woman he's married to!' Now your audience is smiling and you've established an immediate rapport with them. Now that you have their attention, don't let it go.

Chapter 8
When You Arrive

The best way to escape from your problem is to solve it.
Robert Anthony (1916–)

When you take a booking to do a speech, enquire about parking availability. Request in advance that a spot be kept for you near the entry of the venue so that if you're carrying books, tapes, CDs or other material you don't have to carry them too far. It can be useful to have a portable 'luggage cart' to make carrying your props easier.

When you're set to make a speech it's important to arrive at the venue early so you can settle in. This will enable you to check whether everything is going to plan and the organisers are in control. Upon arriving, locate the organiser or 'speaker seeker' as quickly as possible and ask to be taken to the room where you're speaking so that you can check the equipment and set up. This will help calm any nerves because you can ensure that no glitches occur at this early stage of the game. When you first arrive at the venue, check the following:

- **The layout of the room:** Are any of the seats or tables being blocked by pot plants or columns?
- **The lighting:** Are you facing an open window that is letting in direct and strong light?
- **The acoustics:** What is the public address (PA) system like? Is there someone on hand if problems arise?
- **The lectern and microphone:** Are they in good working order?
- **Overhead projector:** Is it positioned correctly?
- **Whiteboard/blackboard:** Are chalk or marking pens available?

- **Flip chart:** Are there coloured pens and do they work?
- **Movie projector:** Are there spare bulbs? Test the film to make sure it has been rewound if it was used earlier in the day.
- **Handouts:** Are there sufficient handouts to go round if the number of attendees has increased?
- Is there a small table near where you're speaking for you to place extra notes and textbooks?
- Are there folding chairs at the side of the room if unexpected people wish to attend?
- Locate the person introducing you and make sure they have your introduction with them. If not, give them a spare copy. Go over it with them to make sure they are comfortable with it.
- Has a a jug of un-iced water and a glass been supplied for you?

Once these initial details are taken care of, it's time to meet members of the audience. Meeting audience members is very important because you can gauge their mood and their expectations before you begin your speech. The personal contact they have with you will make them more responsive and open to you before you start speaking. The best way to do this is to stand by the table where attendees are registering, or at the entry door if it's a less formal function. Smile, introduce yourself, and shake hands. There is no better way to form a connection with your audience than at this one-on-one level.

When everyone has arrived, walk around from group to group and chat so that when you go up on stage to speak, they'll feel they already know you. Sometimes you can pick up a point and work it into your speech. For instance, someone might say they drove for nine hours to hear you speak today, and you could use this when opening your speech: 'I don't know who had the most trouble getting here today. I thought I had it tough when I had to fly three hours to get here, but John Blackmore tells me he had to drive over dirt roads for nine hours.

The other advantage of mixing and mingling like this is that you will meet people who are really excited to hear what you have to say, so when your gaze falls on someone who is glaring at you, move away and try to locate that friendly face. You'll be less inclined to feel nervous too because you've humanised your audience, so instead of looking down at a sea of unknown faces, you'll see them as individuals you were chatting to just a few minutes ago.

WHERE SHOULD YOU STAND?

If you're not speaking with notes and don't need to stand behind a lectern, get out, and stand closer to your audience. Move from the centre of the stage to the left, pause and speak, and then move back to the centre, speak, and then move to the right. This way you'll address all the audience and work the whole area of the stage, not just by physically moving around, but also with your eyes, your arm movements and your voice.

If you're using visuals, use a laser pointer to indicate where you're at, but move away from the screen and stand back. Look at the screen, make your point, and then direct your attention back to the audience.

Take charge of the space you're in—in doing so, you're taking control of the audience. Pull them in to you, take possession of the stage, of the audience, and make them a part of what you're saying.

BE INNOVATIVE BUT...BE CAREFUL

Skipping on to the stage, turning somersaults, juggling balls, wearing a zany mask, or brandishing a sword or sparklers may be dramatically different—but it may also result in you tripping as you skip, falling as you somersault, or it just might make the audience question why you need to do this at all! A memorable presentation doesn't benefit from 'trick' openings—make your entrance with self-assurance and with energy, but remember, you're a speaker, so stand up and wow them with your stage presence, your message and the powerful delivery of that message— and leave the tricks to circus performers.

Chapter 9

How to Develop a Profile

*I may not have gone where I intended to go, but I think that
I have ended up where I intended to be.*

Douglas Adams (1952–2001)

If you're starting out on a professional speaking career it's wise to
perfect your presentation at 'free of fee' engagements before you
offer it to a paying organisation. There are hundreds of charities,
service organisations (Apex, Rotary and Lions), Old Girls' or
Boys' School Unions and local government groups like the
Chamber of Commerce, who have no finances to pay for speakers
and are grateful to those who don't charge. Any of these organisations are useful for honing your public speaking skills and
developing your confidence.

If it's possible to take someone with you, such as a friend or
colleague, ask them to sit in the back row so they can hear how
your voice is carrying, as many of these organisations have either
no public address system, or old ones that are poor in quality.
Turn this to your advantage to see how well you can do if a
microphone doesn't work—which can happen. You need to be
able to improvise.

Ask your support person to gauge audience reaction to your
anecdotes, your jokes, the length of your talk, and your body
language. Then ask them to critique you in what worked and
what didn't work. And you need to accept the criticism, both
negative and positive, and not shoot the messenger. You may need
to work on your script to omit jokes that barely raised a laugh or
were too narrow for a wide audience and shorten any long-

winded segments. You may have developed irritating mannerisms that they can point out to you, such as too many 'ahs' or 'ums' or that you tend to concentrate on one side of the audience rather than 'work the whole room'. An impartial observer will pick up things you would not otherwise be aware of.

How Do You Approach Organisers?

The telephone book, the Internet and Chamber of Commerce or Tourist Information Offices will have a list of organisations that require speakers. Sometimes you will come across the address of the head office and you may have to ring them for details of the local branch. Contact the 'speaker seeker' and either start a manual filing system or use a database system, such as Act Symantec, or a spreadsheet to record every contact you make.

Act Symantec has an excellent 'history' section where you can note when you sent a letter, to whom you sent it, and what response you received. If, for instance, the 'speaker seeker' tells you they have already booked their speakers for the year, you might suggest they keep you in mind should someone fall ill. If, on the other hand, they ask you to ring back in a week as a new 'speaker seeker' is taking over, use the alarm system on your computer to remind you to make the call, or put it in your calendar.

All approaches should be sent by letter, as even if the organisation can't use you this year, the letters are often handed on from one 'speaker seeker' to the next. Similarly, if you do well at their function, organisers will frequently pass on your name and details to their sister group in the next suburb; or a guest at the function who enjoys your presentation may ask you for your card to invite you to speak at their favourite charity or club. You'll be surprised how quickly your database will grow.

Make sure you write a thankyou note to anyone who has taken the trouble to notify other groups about you. I would suggest having a postcard printed, rather than a standard business card. This can have your name, photograph, your topic and contact details on the front, and you can write a short note on the left-hand side on the back, and the address on the right. Organisers are more inclined to keep a card like this in their records than a standard A4 letter, and you'll find you often get a telephone call for a job two or three years after sending out your card. Make sure you enter the name of the person who referred you on your 'booking sheet' (see Sample Letter to Non-fee paying Organisation), as it may not be the same person you sent the card to and you need to thank them.

It's worth the time, effort and possible expense of designing an impressive letterhead and buying good quality paper. You want to appear professional and experienced and writing a letter by hand on lined paper will not do this for you.

Sample Letter to Non-fee Paying Organisations

14th July XXXX

Mr John Nancourt,
Speaker Seeker
Jimwartle Chamber of Commerce
PO Box 1000
Jimwartle NSW 2036

Dear Mr Nancourt,

I would like to offer my speaking services to the Jimwartle Chamber of Commerce at one of your forthcoming Coffee and Muffin Mornings.

At 52 years of age, I was shocked to be made redundant after 22 years as general manager of the Semiconductor Division of Sintorp. I found it impossible to find work, being told that I was 'too old' and virtually 'unemployable'. After some months of despair and a growing sense of worthlessness, I started to put together the pieces and, somewhat reluctantly, felt the only route open to me was to be self-employed, so I opened my own consultancy business.

That was just three years ago and I worked alone from the table in our dining room, unsure of whether I had enough 'steam left in me' to do it. The company now has 11 employees and an annual turnover of $3 million.

My topic is 'There *is* Life after Redundancy' and I feel that what I have to say would be of considerable interest to your members, many of whom may well be wondering what to do when their formal working lives come to an end.

I am aware of the fact that the Chamber of Commerce is a non-fee paying organisation, but it would be my pleasure to speak to your members as I really do believe I have something to offer.

I look forward to hearing from you,

Yours sincerely

TOM SMITH

P.S. Enclosures

WHAT ELSE SHOULD YOU SEND?

When sending out a letter to organisers, you should also include:
- Your curriculum vitae (CV), or details of your professional history to show your credentials and expertise in your field.
- A brief biography about yourself (this can be posted on your website and used to introduce you at the function.)
- Referrals from other non-fee paying groups or professional organisations, or companies where you have spoken, or
- A sales brochure—this combines the CV and the biography and can be posted out to a prospective client, or it can be left on seats at a conference to generate future work. It should have:
    a. your logo
    b. your name
    c. a photograph of yourself
    d. contact information including your website
    e. the title or titles of your presentation with a brief description of the various presentations you do
    f. a list of previous clients for whom you have spoken and perhaps a brief testimonial from them.
    g. a guarantee if you give one—for instance, if you believe that participants who attend your course will definitely be able to do X, Y and Z and if they can't, you will refund your fee. You would need to be able to depend on the integrity of the organisers, however, or the individuals, before deciding to do this.
    h. a list of your products for sale, if applicable.

If you decide to have a brochure printed, ensure a business card can be attached to it. If an agent sends it out, they can insert their card. Agents are reluctant to forward material to a prospective client that has your details on it, as the client is then able to approach you directly. Another solution is to have half the brochures printed with your details and the other half with your agent's.

GOING FROM 'FREE TO FEE'

If no one knows about you, you won't get bookings, so it becomes important at this stage of your speaking career to become highly visible—to become known as an expert in your field. You need to establish yourself as an identity—to position yourself in the speaking marketplace—so that corporations can locate you and book you. It's easy to develop a profile if you follow these simple steps:

- Write articles for business or trade magazines. Initially, you may not be paid, but request that your name and your website be included. As you become better known, you can request a photograph at the top of the article. This will start branding you.
- Write comments for the editorial page of newspapers—again include your name and your email address.
- Write media releases and send them to television, radio and print media. Generate as many interviews as you can to create interest around you and your topic.
- Arrange public seminars and workshops—those who attend will go away and talk about you. Let the press know who you are and give free tickets to them so that they attend your speech and write about you.
- Combine with one or two other experts or speaking colleagues and arrange a seminar that showcases all of you. This way you cast the net wider and attract a broader audience.
- Ask attendees at any event where you speak to drop their business cards in a box and offer your product (e.g. book, CD, tape) or a bottle of wine (preferably with your own label) as prizes.

You can then use the business cards to build up your database. The first public seminars and workshops you organise may be hard to fill, but if you offer a specially reduced rate to those who are already on your database (if they bring a colleague or friend), you'll find succeeding functions easier to book out.

- Offer your services as a speaker to a major hotel chain like the Hilton or Sheraton, which arranges regular business breakfasts. They generally advertise the function in their quarterly brochures. Make sure you email a photograph to accompany the advertisement.

- Write a book—not only can you sell this at your seminars and workshops, thus defraying costs, but a book gives you another opportunity to generate more publicity.

- Join clubs, networking groups and attend as many functions as possible to expand your circle of acquaintances. You may be required to stand up and introduce yourself. Make sure you have something interesting to say that mentions what you do. It's excellent advertising and will help you to become known in your field as an expert.

- Join specific interest groups, for instance, Rostrum, Toastmasters or National Speakers of Australia, where you can attend meetings and conferences and meet mentors and experienced speakers who will guide you in the early stages of your career.

Step by step you're positioning yourself in the marketplace as an authority; a credible person who knows what they are talking about. The more the general public knows about you, the more you'll come to the attention of 'speaker seekers'.

How to Generate Publicity

In order to maximise your speaking at a function or at one of your own workshops or seminars, approach local newspapers including the 'free press' (the newspapers delivered weekly or monthly at no charge). For this you will need a media release, your photograph (preferably as a Jpeg file) that you can email to the journalist, and a brief biography written in Word that they can cut and paste. If you write the article yourself, journalists will be more inclined to use it, as it involves no extra work for them. They have very heavy workloads and are not looking for more.

It's also worth contacting both the local community and commercial radio stations. They are often looking for interest stories and the more that people hear about you the better. In addition, those who are not able to attend on the day may make a note of who you are and what you speak about, and contact you for future work. It's important to leave a business card with the receptionist at the radio station so that if someone rings up and asks about 'the man who started his own consultancy business' or 'the woman who was talking about her new book about budgies', the receptionist is able to refer to your card and pass on your details.

It is also important to write thankyou notes to the journalist who interviews you for the print media, and to anyone who interviews you on the radio—and their producer as well if there is one. It's likely that they will keep your card and contact you in the future if they are looking for someone to comment on something within your field of expertise. You're on your way to being regarded as an expert and your opinion being sought will give you more airtime, and therefore more chance of being heard by someone who will book you for a talk—preferably a paid one.

How to Write a Media Release

When writing a media release, use A4 coloured paper (but not so dark that the text is hard to read) for the version you plan to mail out, and white paper for the versions you intend to fax to clients. Use letterhead and always date your release. If you don't want any information released before a certain date, for example, the names of winners in a competition, put an embargo date very clearly at the top of the page in big bold type.

A clear and concise media release is usually one page in length with a catchy title. You should use lower-case text in a 12-point font with italics or bold type used for keywords or phrases, and the most important points should be at the top of the release. For example, if you're promoting your book launch, *what* the function is, *where* it is, *why* it's being held, *how* much it will cost, and *who* to contact for details are listed first. Then, further down, list the less important information. This way if a journalist is in a hurry, at least they get the gist of your media release; they'll determine their level of interest by the first couple of paragraphs, so pack them with punch! For added interest, use quotes. For example, 'Dr Smythe, a leading American asthma specialist visiting Brisbane this week, warned that, "Medihalers used indiscriminately in children under the age of five can cause instant death".' The advantage of doing this is that you gain credibility by quoting an authority, and injecting dialogue adds interest by breaking up the prose.

Make sure that you add the contact details of people who can supply further comments. For example, 'Penny Sullivan can be contacted on 5577 8895 or on her mobile 0404 789 569 to discuss the repercussions of Dr Smythe's disturbing report'. If possible, give two people who can comment, in case the media can't reach you personally when they want to.

Be prepared to take media calls as you're serving up a hot dinner or getting out of the shower! You want them more than they want you.

WHAT PHOTOGRAPHS DO YOU NEED?

It's worth having photographs of yourself professionally done to get the best results. Look at photographs in magazines and newspapers to see which ones impress you and copy their style. A professional photographer will guide you with what colours photograph best and with the aid of lighting you can be sure to look your best.

For a woman, make sure your hairstyle is 'of today' so that you look modern and can relate to a younger audience as well as those in your own age group. If you wear glasses, ensure they are the right shape and colour and don't dominate the photograph. For a man, if you have longish hair, it should be clean and tied back. If you have a beard or moustache, make sure they're trimmed.

When handing out photographs of yourself, it's best to give prospective clients:

- A head shot with a plain background—in black-and-white and colour.
- A full body shot with interest, for example, if you're a dog trainer, perhaps be surrounded by four of five different breeds of dogs to indicate that your method of training applies to all breeds. Supply the photograph in black-and-white and colour.

RSRSR Formula

The Ring, Send, Ring, Send, Ring, (RSRSR) Formula is a way to get people to notice you. First *ring* the radio station, newspaper or television channel and speak to the person to whom you are sending the media release. The advantage of this is that they'll soon tell you if they're the right person, and if they're not they can re-direct you to who is. Once you have the right person:

- Introduce yourself.
- State briefly what it is you're sending.
- Whet their appetite by telling them what your presentation is called, for example, 'Death for five-year-olds', so they will recognise your release when it comes through.
- Ask if they have a direct fax line.
- Ask for their email address.
- Send the release to both the producer and the presenter by

either fax or email (the release may not 'grab' the producer, but the presenter may love it, or vice versa).

- Wait no more than two days before ringing again and ask the recipient if they received your media release. If they didn't receive it, send it again and then ring again!

Being successful with the media is like filling a dish with layers upon layers of lasagne—you keep calling and sending until you can't call or send any more.

How to Pick the Best Time to Make Contact

If you're dealing with radio, such as a breakfast program which goes off the air at 9.00 am, you'll need to get on the phone at 8.50 am and stay online, holding until the presenter comes off the air. You may even have to do this three mornings in a row as the presenter often leaves the studio and is out of the building in three minutes flat. Some stay to discuss tomorrow's program with their producer, but for those who've been in the studio since 3.00 am preparing the program for a 6.00am start, they can't wait to get out of there.

Similarly with television, if you're following up by phone, don't ring the program to follow up your media release just before they go to air. Use your commonsense and ask whoever answers the phone when is a good time to speak to the producer (or the researcher).

Always retain your composure no matter how many times you're shoved from pillar to post. Remember, the editorial you'll gain will be invaluable in dollar terms.

The Value of a Website

Regard your website as being a core component of your success as a speaker. Most companies, clients and speaking agents will find you in this way—not to mention the media if they're looking for an expert to make a comment on their program or for their newspaper or magazine. Clients can take your photograph, biography and product or book information from your website, and this saves you valuable time in answering phone calls or email queries.

Decide on what you want your website to say about you and keep it simple. Determine who your target audience is and then make it interactive if that suits your purpose (and your product), but make sure it's linked to other sites where potential clients can find you.

How to Handle Media Interviews

In every interview, it is important to choose your words carefully, be concise, speak in phrases (the media in general are fond of a quip or quote of say 15 to 20 seconds in length), so don't waffle or get side-tracked.

Go into the interview knowing in advance the main points you want to make. If you're in Darwin, but hope to promote your seminars in Melbourne the following month, make sure you get that in and the fact that you are only there for one night. So rather than saying, 'When I come to town next month' say, 'When I come to Melbourne in June I'll only be there for the night of the 7th before I leave for Adelaide ...' Similarly, if you're promoting a book you've written, don't say, 'When I wrote the book I had no idea it would generate such controversy' but rather, 'When I wrote *To Kill or Not To Kill,* I had no idea it would generate so much controversy' so that you get the title of the book in the interview at least once.

If you think the interviewer won't have any idea of who you are or your subject, you may care to email them some background information before the interview takes place. Take a copy of those suggestions on the day of the interview in case your email went astray, was disregarded, never received, or left in a briefcase. Following are some techniques to use in different media interviews.

PRINT

Being interviewed for a newspaper or magazine can be tricky in that most journalists today don't use shorthand and sometimes discrepancies and errors can occur. Some journalists use a tape recorder, but even so, a long interview has to be cut down to a specific number of words. Magazines can have a four-month lead time, but newspaper interviews usually appear within a day or so of the interview.

RADIO

Interviews can be 'live to air' (that is, you go into the studio and speak to the presenter and it is broadcast simultaneously), or 'pre-recorded' (in which you may still go to the studio, and the interviewer will tape the interview to play at a later time or day). Both 'live to air' and 'pre-recorded' interviews can be done by telephone. With 'pre-records' there can be some slicing or editing to fit a time slot, so there is always a risk of being quoted out of context.

Remember that your listeners will not be experts in your field so you need to speak in language that they'll understand, that is, colloquial (conversational, chatty) English. It helps if you try to imagine you're speaking to a particular person so that your style is natural and not contrived. Have an amusing quote or anecdote at the ready (time it beforehand so you know its 20 to 30 seconds long), as the people who are listening may be driving a car, doing the ironing or eating their breakfast. You need to be entertaining and informative in a short space of time.

TELEVISION

This is a very immediate medium and gives you an opportunity to express yourself with eye contact, smiling, hand gestures and voice inflection. Interviews can be cut so be aware of every word you use lest it be taken out of context. The main point with any interview is to ask questions beforehand about the audience profile so that you can prepare key points that will interest those listeners. Remember to use clear and concise sentences. Statistics should only be sprinkled through the interview and, if possible, try to inject a little light-hearted humour so that the interview does have some entertainment value to it.

For television, your appearance is very important. The way you dress, your hairstyle and makeup (whether male or female), your mannerisms, how you're sitting and your facial expressions are constantly being watched. Your appearance should be commensurate with the reason you're being interviewed. For example, if you're speaking on behalf of your organisation, business dress would be appropriate, but if you're being interviewed about a boat race and you're on the deck of the boat, casual clothing would be more suitable. Fine stripes or bold checks can sometimes be a problem, as they seem to 'move' on screen. Women should avoid dangling earrings or very shiny jewellery, which captures the strong studio lights. If you're unsure of what colour to wear, ring the producer and ask what colour the set is (particularly the chairs), as you don't want to wear a bright red suit if you're sitting on a bright red sofa.

If you feel that you do your own makeup well, you can do this beforehand to save time, but the makeup artist at the studio will usually powder your face and add just a little colour or emphasis where necessary. For men, the makeup artist may feel you need a light powdering if you have a very ruddy complexion or shiny, sweaty skin.

Once filming has begun, pretend the camera isn't there and speak to the interviewer as if the two of you are chatting informally in your lounge room. Sit straight in the chair; don't perch on the edge or you'll look nervous and apprehensive. The technician will attach a microphone to your clothing, so it's important to wear either a jacket, a blouse or a dress that opens down the front, as the fine cords are usually taken up inside the jacket so they're out of sight. The small microphone at the end is then attached to the top of the blouse or on the lapel of the jacket. Sit comfortably and check that your skirt is tucked down or your trouser leg hasn't risen up over your socks. Remember not to fiddle with your collar or twist a curl of hair, or take your spectacles on and off as all these movements are irritating to the viewer. Hand gestures should be kept to a minimal because sometimes things can be exaggerated on television. If you're speaking directly to the camera, try to imagine this is a person you know and speak to them, as stiff facial expressions can make you look nervous or 'shifty'. Ask before the interview begins how much time you have and this will give you an idea of what you want to say first so that you can prioritise your comments.

> Don't be greedy and try to turn an interview into a commercial. To do so means that you will never get on the program again. Keep your answers brief and interesting and the producer will call you next time for a pertinent comment!

How to Boost Your Expertise

You need to read a wide range of national, and if possible, international newspapers. Watch different channels and listen to different programs on different radio stations, then use this information to your advantage to boost your expertise.

If, for example, you were in the staff selection or management consultancy arena and you read an important article stating that researchers have found that it only takes 30 seconds to make a first impression, you could write a media release on this, angling it towards the importance of presentation at job interviews. If you are in the image consultancy field or run a deportment school, you could angle this to indicate that young people should really learn how to walk and how to sit etc. Use your imagination and think outside the square.

THE ROLE OF THE AGENT

The role of a speaker's agent or speaker's bureau is to secure paid speaking engagements. Some charge an up-front annual fee to register while others only charge a percentage of each engagement. Agents can request that all paid work and media enquiries be directed through their office. This means that if you're speaking at a function and are approached by another organisation to speak for them, this enquiry must be directed to your speaker's bureau and a percentage of the fee is paid to the agent. Agents and bureaus can also offer other services to assist you in your career as a speaker, such as:

- Consulting
- Coaching and mentoring
- Media contract negotiation
- Personalities for commercials
- Professional presenters for corporate videos
- Entertainment packages for clubs and conventions.

Agents and speakers' bureaus can specialise in booking speakers who are experts in finance and business, sporting personalities or celebrities.

HOW TO FIND AN AGENT

This is not easy because many agents don't want new clients, particularly those without a proven track record or high profile. The best way is to ask other speakers if they are satisfied with the service their speaker's bureau is providing or try searching under 'speaker's agent' or 'speaker's bureau' on the Internet.

Chapter 10

Different Kinds of Speakers

Everyone is kneaded out of the same dough but not baked in the same oven.

Yiddish proverb

Public speaking takes many forms: an MC at a company dinner or wedding, whose role is to ensure that the function runs smoothly; the motivational speaker whose aim is to arouse and motivate an audience; the lecturer whose role is to teach; and the guest speaker, who being an authority on a topic, wants to inform. In addition, a speaker may be someone detailing an annual report, introducing or thanking another speaker, presenting or receiving an award, or someone who has been invited to stand up and 'say a few words' at a moment's notice.

What Does an MC Do?

An MC can be a *professional* employed by an event organiser or wedding reception house for a company dinner, wedding, conference, or Christmas party to ensure that the function runs smoothly and that any glitches that occur are dealt with quickly and unobtrusively. An MC can also be an *amateur*—a friend or godparent of a couple being married—who is invited to direct proceedings at a wedding, engagement or 21st birthday party.

The MC is like the oil that lubricates a car—it is their job to make sure that everything runs smoothly. They are behind-the-scenes people who are chosen for their calm and composed manner, so that if a crisis occurs, they will immediately handle it. For example, if the band doesn't arrive on time, or the best man is so drunk he has to be taken out and locked in the car, the MC finds recorded music and gets another groomsman to stand in for the disgraced best man. It is also their role to make sure that the PA system works and that the speakers stay sober and don't go over time or tell risqué jokes which may have the bride in tears. They also keep an eye on the clock and act like the conductor in an orchestra, telling people what to do and when. They may need to tell the band to turn down the volume, or the drink waiters to stop serving wine to a boisterous table; they need to remind the bride when it's time to change into her 'going away' clothes, and for the bridesmaids to hand out the wedding cake.

The MC must make sure before the event that everyone knows their role for the night and then they make sure that they fulfil it. A meeting before the event with the main players is advised, as is having a list of the jobs for the night, so that in all the excitement no one or nothing is overlooked. An MC needs to be a person who is organised and reliable with an air of authority, so that when they give an instruction or make a decision, it is followed—they are virtually a bridge linking the various stages of an event. For instance, they may introduce a speaker, and while that person is speaking they are instructing the waiters on when to pour the champagne for the bridal toast, while at the same time checking that the knife is beside the wedding cake ready for cutting.

At a formal dinner, the MC will act as a shepherd herding the flock into the dining room. It is the MC who announces that dinner is about to be served and guides the guests to their tables. If someone has been left off a table and has nowhere to sit, the MC will rearrange another table and squeeze them in. The MC says a few words to welcome the hosts and the guests in a brief speech, proposes the toast to the Queen, if there is to be one, and introduces the minister, priest or rabbi to say grace or bless the meal if that is required.

A competent MC will make sure that everyone is in the right place at the right time to do whatever it is they have to do—and will also provide a few words to link up the speakers so there is no deadly silence when one speaker is leaving the stage and another is coming up. They may like to go prepared with a few little anecdotes to use as 'fillers' if something goes wrong, but the role of the MC is not to be an entertainer, but a coordinator. It is very poor form for an MC to upstage or 'steal the thunder' of any of the speakers.

If the audience is rather lively, the MC will need to settle them down so that speakers can be heard, and if a speaker does run over time, the MC will need to move surreptitiously on to the stage and discreetly wind them up. The MC must thank each speaker and then introduce the next. If the audience is looking a little gloomy at the end of a heavy day of workshops and seminars, the MC might need to tell a couple of amusing stories to lighten the mood and create a more festive occasion.

In a crisis, the MC has to be ready with some impromptu ad-libbing and be able to move the event on so that the audience is unaware of what has happened. Another prerequisite of this role is the ability to control an audience and to appear confident at all times. It's a fact of life that no one notices when everything goes smoothly, but everyone is aware when something goes wrong, so the MC needs to be very self-assured to deal with crises and glitches and to close the event on a high note with thanks to the hosts, the guests, musicians, and the wait staff, who have all worked so hard to make the event the success it has been.

Anyone planning to be an MC *must* learn how to hold and use a microphone correctly. If you cannot be heard or understood, no one will take any notice of you and you will have no control over the proceedings.

What is a
Motivational Speaker?

The aim of a motivational speaker is to inspire, change and 'spur into action' their audience. They must persuade their audience to their own point of view using humour, imagery, storytelling, drama and passion. Their speech can be either very subtle in its persuasiveness to gradually swing the audience to their point of view, or it can be overtly persuasive and appeal to the emotions of the audience and have immediate impact.

What is a Lecturer?

The aim of a lecturer is to inform, reveal and explain by teaching something to the audience that they didn't previously know. A lecture should contain many facts, ideas, figures and perhaps statistics which need to be arranged in such a way that the audience can follow the information and draw inferences and conclusions from it. The success of a lecture depends on the clarity and simplicity with which these ideas are given and the personality and presentation skills of the lecturer. There is no such thing as a dull topic, just a dull presenter, so the lecturer needs to inject some wit, humour, relevant light-hearted material, and above all, enthusiasm for the subject matter.

What is a Guest Speaker?

This term is used for someone who is an authority on a topic (for example, the breeding habits of horses), who has an important role in public life, or is very successful in the commercial world and therefore is of interest to specific groups. For example, the Minister for Education could be invited to be a guest speaker at a school end of year speech day, or an ex-diplomat could be invited to speak on world affairs to a media club, or an author could be invited to speak about their new book to university students majoring in English literature.

How to Invite, Introduce and Thank a Speaker

As the host of an event or presentation, you may need to invite, introduce and thank a professional public speaker. You may be someone who has never spoken in public before (and who has been dreading doing so since waking that morning). If this is you, remember that your thanks should be brief. You are not there to tell long-winded stories that match, or even worse, outshine those of the speaker. You *are* required, however, to pronounce their name correctly, and that of their book or name of their company. If you're appointed by your company or organisation to be the person to arrange for a guest speaker, then it's up to you to:

- Contact the speaker beforehand.
- Confirm the time, venue and details.
- Ask the speaker what, if anything, they will need.
- Confirm publicity or promotional arrangements.
- Organise any equipment they may require.
- Attend to any flight booking and accommodation if necessary.
- Ask if there is anything the speaker cannot eat if they are staying for a meal after their speech.
- Tell the speaker the numbers of guests attending.
- Remind the speaker to forward an autobiography for a correct introduction.
- Find out whether the speaker has invited any celebrity guests.

- Arrange parking near the entrance of the venue in case the speaker has to carry charts, books, flyers and so on.
- Go out and meet the speaker and escort him or her inside—show them around and ensure that they have a drink and are introduced to someone who will 'take care of them' until it is time for their presentation. It is unforgivable to allow a guest speaker to stand lost and alone, knowing no one, until it's time for him or her to speak.
- Make sure that any equipment you're responsible for providing, such as an overhead projector or flip chart, works and that it's correctly positioned on the stage.
- Appoint someone to 'move' the vote of thanks (see page 100) on behalf of the audience.
- Ensure that the speaker is paid promptly, and that any out-of-pocket expenses they may have incurred are included in your payment.

Sample Letter to Invite a Guest Speaker

13 January 20XX

Dr Laurence Danner
Little Paws Veterinary Surgery
22 Carinya Street
Moorooka Qld 4061

Dear Dr Danner,

Protect Our Pets is a not-for-profit organisation, which was founded in 1980 to help relocate stray or abandoned pets throughout Australia. We have a number of corporate sponsors in industries ranging from pet food manufacturing to communications and have over 1000 members nationwide.

Our annual Pets for People campaign, a four-week effort to 'match' pets to needy owners—people with physical or intellectual disabilities—kicks off on Wednesday 23 August 20XX with a breakfast. We aim to have a veterinarian speak to our members and guests for approximately 30 minutes on general pet care, and hope that you'll be able to fill that role for us. The breakfast is to be held at Oxley's Restaurant at 7.00 am on 4 September 20XX.

You have an excellent reputation within the veterinary field, having being referred to us by last year's speaker, Dr Christopher Stevens, and we'd be delighted to have you on our program.

Please let me know if you are able to attend by 13 February 20XX. I look forward to hearing from you.

Sincerely,

(Ms) Susan Burraston
Managing Director

How to Introduce a Guest Speaker

To introduce a guest speaker, find out something about them in advance so that you can make the appropriate introduction. Check their name so you can pronounce it and use their correct title—Dr, Professor, the Right Honourable etc. Next state the title of the presentation and then say a few words to show how the speech is relevant, for instance:

'We're very fortunate to have Dr Danner with us today to talk about his research in discoid lupus erythematosus (DLE). With 17 cases of this rare disease suddenly presenting at hospitals every day all over the country, this new strain is something we all need to be aware of.'

You now have the audience's interest. It's worthwhile keeping a file on the speakers you've either seen in action or invited to your company event. This way you will remember which speakers you found exceptionally interesting or talented and have their contact details on hand so that you can invite them back again. You should record:

- the speaker's name, qualifications and contact details
- the day and date you saw them speak (on each occasion)
- the topic of the speech (again for each occasion)
- what you did and didn't like about the speech or the speaker
- how much you paid the speaker
- any particular requests the speaker made (such as that fruit be provided in their dressing room)
- where they stayed while on circuit with your company seminar (if applicable)
- their publicist's or personal assistant's name.

If you're organising a meeting or function where a speaker is to address the audience you should:

- introduce the speaker
- maintain order
- supervise questions from the audience
- either thank the speaker yourself, or appoint someone else to do so.

You may need to get the attention of the audience, so a small bell can be useful, otherwise tap a glass with a spoon. You may need to say 'Order!' a couple of times if the audience is rowdy. Having done that, you should then introduce the speaker and welcome them on behalf of the audience (in no more than 200 words):

'I must say I'm delighted to note the wonderful attendance we have here tonight—not that I'm surprised when we have such a remarkable man as John Turnbull to address us.' (Pause and look at the speaker as the audience may choose to applaud here, then look back to the audience.) 'I know that John needs very little introduction to you in regard to his research on the cause of crime today, but let me just bring you up to date with some of John's latest achievements.' (Read John's autobiography.) 'Would you please welcome John Turnbull.' (Lead the applause and then sit down as John Turnbull goes to the lectern.)

How to Finish a Speech

When the speaker/s have completed their speech, it is time to wind up the proceedings and appoint someone to 'move' the vote of thanks. The chairman usually does this and should rise, go to the lectern and say something like:

> 'Thank you John. You've painted a chilling picture but I'm sure everyone here holds out that same hope. I know you will all join me in thanking John for giving up his time to speak to us tonight.'

The chairman should then lead the audience in applause and if the speaker has agreed to answer questions, then the chairman might say:

> 'John has agreed to take questions. Unfortunately, time only permits three or four, so could I have a show of hands please.'

It's up to the chairman to oversee questions. Remember that if another speaker (or a meal) is waiting, it's discourteous to run over time. Questions are asked through the chairman, not directly to the speaker; for example, 'Mr Chairman, I'd like to ask John ...' or, 'Mr Chairman, I wonder whether John would tell us ...'

This formula gives the chairman the chance to disallow a question that might be tasteless or embarrassing to the speaker. It's up to the chairman to ask the speaker if he's willing to answer any sensitive questions. If there are no questions asked from the floor, the chairman himself may like to pose one on behalf of the audience, for instance, 'I'm sure, John, that all our members here tonight would love to know ...' When the questions are over, the chairman should again say:

> 'Thank you again, John, I'm sure that's cleared up a lot of grey areas for everyone here tonight. I now call on Duncan McKenzie to move a vote of thanks.'

It's important to note that you don't 'give' a vote of thanks; it's 'moved' by the entire audience, and not just by the one person who articulates it, so the 'mover' should always make that clear.

How to Move a Vote of Thanks

A representative of the host usually moves the vote of thanks. They should go to the rostrum and make it clear that they accept the privilege of thanking the speaker on behalf of the audience. They must thank the speaker for finding the time to attend the function and tell them how much it means to the audience to have this opportunity to hear them speak. (The 'mover' should look at the speaker as they say this.) The 'mover' should try to pick out one or two interesting points the speaker has made, such as a statistic or a striking fact to mention, for example:

> 'I must say John astonished me, as I'm sure he did every-one tonight, with some of those statistics. To think that crime has increased tenfold in the last 18 months is very disturbing indeed.'

He should then call on the audience to carry the vote of thanks by applause:

> 'Ladies and gentlemen, will you join me in thanking John for his most informative speech.'

Everyone should clap at this point.

If you're called upon to move the vote of thanks, don't make it too short in case it seems like an empty gesture. You should write about 200 words and most of it, except for the one or two specific points, can be written beforehand.

Sample of Vote of Thanks

'Mr Chairman, ladies and gentlemen, we hear a lot of speakers during the course of the year, and we cover a lot of topics. But I'm sure everyone here would agree with me when I say that your address, John, (look at John) is without a doubt the most illuminating and interesting I can recall. None of us likes to admit that crime is increasing in our community, but to hear from you tonight not only the reasons, but some of the possible solutions, is refreshing and encouraging to say the least.

'We thank you not only for giving up your time—and we know you have very little of it—to join us here this

> evening, but for all the hard work you're doing to get our
> community back on track. We're even more grateful to
> you for giving us some tangible solutions as to how we
> can help solve the problem. Ladies and gentlemen, I ask
> you to join with me in thanking John Turnbull.'

The audience applauds once the vote of thanks is complete, and if the
guest is to be given a gift, it will be handed to them by the person who
moved the vote of thanks. Then, both the speaker and the chairperson
will leave the lectern area. If this speech has been part of a meeting,
the chairperson would usually add, 'I now declare this meeting closed.'

THANKING A GUEST SPEAKER

A 'thankyou' note to a guest speaker has a dual purpose: firstly, to
show your appreciation to them for giving up their time and
sharing their knowledge; and secondly, many speakers like to
keep a file of 'testimonials' to show to prospective clients.

Sample Thankyou Note to the Guest Speaker

18 August 20XX

32 Campbell Parade
Chelsea NSW 2345

Dear John,

I want to congratulate you on behalf of the Australian
Journalists' Association for your address to us on crime
last night.

Your speech was one of the most enlightening and
instructive that we've heard on the subject of increasing

crime levels in the suburbs, and I must say that I feel much more confident having heard your comments on the subject.

I should add that there was some very positive feedback about your presentation at the breakfast meeting this morning and many requests for you to return and make a presentation next year if you are agreeable to that. I'll be in touch.

Once again, congratulations on a job well done. You've left us all with much to think about.

Sincerely yours,

Merryn Fulloon

How to Make
an Award Presentation

If you've been asked to make a presentation of some kind, such as an award for long service or a prize, always begin by saying something about the award itself: what it is and what it's being awarded for. This allows you to say something sincere and flattering about why the recipient deserves the award and how delighted you are to be making the presentation. If it's an informal situation, there may well be no microphone, so keep your head up, look around at all sections of the audience to include everyone in your remarks, and speak clearly, for example:

'It is my very real pleasure today to be presenting the UNESCO Peace Prize to Belinda Gordon, who has done a remarkable job this year with her reports from Central Asia. Her work has done a great deal to raise international awareness of the plight of children in war zones all over the world.'

You as the presenter will be holding the trophy or gift and looking at the audience as you are saying this. Then turn and face Belinda and say:

'Belinda, we've read your reports and there could be no more worthy person receiving this prize. You've done a great job and everyone here at Channel 4 is proud of you.'

Now you hand the trophy to Belinda and perhaps, if you know her, kiss her on the cheek. If you don't know her well, then hand her the trophy with your left hand and shake hands with the right. If the prize is awarded as a brooch or pin, you may care to attach it for her.

How to Respond
if You're Receiving an Award

If you are being given an award, you should smile and thank the presenter as you receive it. You should then turn to the audience and say something like:

'I'm just so thrilled to win this. I *have* worked hard this year, but any sacrifices I made to capture the story week after week were very small indeed compared to the sacrifices that children everywhere are making today. Thank you very much UNESCO for providing this award, and thank you everyone at Channel 4 for nominating me. I'll wear this peace brooch with pride.'

The audience will applaud and you should then sit down again or move back into the audience. The main thing to remember is for you to keep your speech short while at the same time sounding genuinely moved and appreciative of whatever you've been given, even if it's something you dislike at first sight. You should always:

- thank the people responsible for making the award, in this case, UNESCO.
- thank the people who have helped you win the award, for instance, any co-workers who nominated you; and,
- thank the person who is making the presentation as they hand you the prize.

If you are receiving an award or gift because you're leaving a firm to go on long service or maternity leave, then you might like to reminisce about the wonderful memories you have of working for that particular company and the special friendships you've made—just don't get carried away! If you're given something ghastly as a gift, don't even hint that you're in shock. Look at it admiringly and say something like:

'I'm really touched that you went to the trouble of finding something like this for our new home and I hope that some of you will find the time to come and visit me when stock-taking is over. Both my husband and I would love to see you. Thank you.'

Make sure you put the gift in a prominent place in your home if a former colleague visits!

CHAPTER II

TOASTS AND HOW TO PROPOSE THEM

There are remarks that sow and remarks that reap.
Ludwig Wittgenstein (1889–1951)

What is a toast? A toast is a short (one minute or less) speech in honour of someone, a group of people or an organisation. What is said needs to suit the occasion, the type of guest present, and be directed to the person being toasted. It's not an opportunity to 'take the floor' or be clever at the expense of the person being toasted.

Being asked to propose a toast is one of the most common reasons why you may have to get up and speak in front of an audience. Weddings, anniversaries and birthday parties are the most popular events for toasts, where friends and family rise to give their well wishes to the people being celebrated. Toasts can be made to foreign guests who are visiting at the time of the event; any officials, dignitaries or government ministers in attendance; the leading partner in any new business deal arising from the event; any friends or colleagues who are leaving or retiring, and conversely any new staff members; elderly members or special guests at your table; anyone who is newly married or has just become a parent for the first time; anyone who has recently been promoted or awarded with an honour; and anyone you feel deserves a special thank you for any reason. Informal toasts, toasts for 18th and 21st birthday parties, anniversaries and weddings, together with their responses are included in this chapter.

When to Propose a Toast

Hopefully, you'll get some warning when you have to propose a toast; but sometimes it may just seem appropriate for someone to get to their feet and say a few words. Whatever the situation, keep it brief—it's not a speech! When beginning a toast, drinking glasses should be filled and people should be on their feet *before* the toast is proposed. Those who don't drink wine can raise a glass of soft drink or water instead. There are two points of the celebration where toasts should be proposed:

- At the beginning of the meal, where the host will often remain seated and make a toast to welcome everyone.
- At the beginning of the dessert course, where the host may propose a toast to the guest of honour. At this time, it is traditional for the host to stand, but the person to whom the toast is being proposed to should remain seated and not drink a toast.

The person who was toasted should then rise and respond with a toast, to which they also may drink. If the occasion is a wedding, this is when other guests might rise and propose toasts of their own. It would be wise for the MC to advise them beforehand on the wisdom of brevity.

Charging (Filling) the Glass

The host should either delegate someone to ensure that everyone has a glass with a drink of some sort in it, or instruct the waiters to fill the glasses. If no waiters are present, guests could be asked to charge their own glasses.

Types of Toasts

Both men and women can initiate toasts to a guest of honour and on all business occasions where food and wine is served, calling a toast is usual. Some of the most common toasts and reasons for toasting are given below.

Loyal Toast

The Loyal Toast, which is still drunk at some functions, is the briefest of all the toasts. The person who makes the toast simply stands and says, 'The Queen' or 'To the Queen' at which the guests stand, raise their glasses and repeat, 'The Queen'. However, at many functions today, the loyal toast is made 'To Australia'. In times gone by, after the Loyal Toast it was permissible to smoke, however, today ashtrays would not be provided at an event like this. Smokers should go outside.

Informal Toast to Someone Joining a Company

The person proposing the toast should stand, tap a glass with his or her spoon or ring a bell to get the attention of the guests, and then say something like:

> 'After 15 exciting and challenging years with Floyd International, it is with enormous pride that I can say I've watched this company grow and it is with great pleasure that I welcome Alistair Gordon to our team. With Alistair working beside us who knows what the next 15 years will bring? To Alistair Gordon.'

Guests will now get to their feet and raise their glasses and everyone will say, 'To Alistair Gordon" *except* Alistair, who will remain seated. Guests will then drink to him. Alistair should smile and say,

'Thank you'. Then, when the guests are seated, Alistair should rise to his feet, turn toward whoever made the toast and say, 'Thank you'. He then should turn to the rest of the guests and say:

> 'I have some "thank-yous" I'd like to make tonight, most of all to those at my previous employer, Strong & Company, who worked so hard with me to produce the enviable sales figures we achieved. They were difficult years and the team spirit we developed is the kind of spirit I would like to see us develop here at Floyd International.
>
> 'My father was an airforce man who loved to tell me it took 10 men on the ground to keep one man in the sky. You're the men and women on the ground and I'm going to need your help to keep me in the sky!
>
> 'I thank you for this welcome tonight and assure you that I look forward to working with you. I'd like to ask you to drink with me to Floyds.'

Everyone will stand and say, 'To Floyds', then Alistair will sit down. How long you want the toast to be depends on the formality of the occasion, how many speakers are to follow, and on how polished a speaker you are, but it shouldn't go over a couple of minutes at most. Avoid telling tales of your first day or any other anecdotes, which, while they may be of great sentimental value to those closest to you, will mean nothing to other guests.

AN 18TH OR 21ST BIRTHDAY PARTY TOAST

The person making the toast at this kind of occasion is usually a relative, such as an uncle or an old friend of the family. The person making the toast should stand, tap a glass with a spoon to get the attention of the other guests and say something like:

'As Jane's only uncle, and as her greatest admirer, I would like to propose a toast on this happy and very special occasion of her 18th birthday. Would you please stand and raise your glasses.'

Guests should now get to their feet, raise their glasses and say, 'To Jane', and Jane should remain seated. The guests will drink but Jane shouldn't. She should smile and say, 'Thank you'. Then, when the guests are seated she can, if she chooses, rise and respond.

How long the toast should be depends on the formality of the occasion, how many speakers are to follow, and on how polished the speaker is, but it should be only a couple of minutes at most. Avoid telling intimate tales or anecdotes, which, while they may be of great sentimental value to close friends and family, will mean nothing to the other guests. If there are genuinely interesting achievements that should be mentioned, they can be referred to, for instance:

'I'm very proud to be the uncle of the first girl to swim the 100 metres in two minutes in the Olympic Games. Jane always was a child we knew would do well, but her success has been greater than we ever imagined. We're very proud indeed and her Aunty Joan and I know you join with us in wishing her all the best for the future.'

Since it is clear that toasts are to be made at this time, someone should be delegated to see that everyone has a glass with some sort of liquid in it. When all the glasses are filled, Jane should rise to her feet, turn toward whoever made the toast and say, 'Thank you'. She should then turn to the rest of her guests and say:

'Thank you Uncle Bob. I have some thank yous I'd like to make tonight too, most of all to my father, without whose skill at maths I would never have passed a maths exam, and my mother who never missed a tuckshop day in all my years at school. I would like to thank my grandparents too for making such a long trip to be with me tonight, and my friends for organising this fabulous party. Thanks to all of you.' (Jane then sits down.)

ENGAGEMENT TOAST

If the engagement party has a buffet meal, keep your toast very short. Remember a lot of female guests may be balancing precariously on stiletto heels! A toast can include something like:

'Both Elizabeth and I would like to thank you for joining us on this very happy occasion of Susan's engagement to David Muir. David is a fine young man and we look forward to welcoming him into our family. I'd also like to thank David's parents for their kind words about Susan earlier this evening. I'm delighted to say that we feel as pleased with our daughter's choice as they do with their son's. So I ask you to raise your glasses and drink to the future happiness of Susan and David.'

Everyone should raise their glasses and say, 'To Susan and David'. Depending on the formality of the occasion, Susan may wish to respond:

'Thank you, Dad. I'd just like to thank both Mum and Dad for hosting this wonderful party for us tonight. It's been a lovely way to meet the rest of David's family and it's the first time all of our friends have been together like this for ages. It's great to see everyone again and I thank you all for coming.'

If she wants to make it a toast as well, Susan could add, 'To Elizabeth and Bill'. Then everyone should repeat, 'To Elizabeth and Bill'.

WEDDING TOASTS

Since many weddings tend to be more informal these days, so are the speeches. It is usual for speeches to be made towards the end of the wedding reception when coffee is being served and before the wedding cake is cut, but some couples now prefer to get them out of the way early. This is a good idea, especially if those making the speeches are apprehensive, as once the toasts are over they can relax and enjoy themselves.

Traditionally, the father of the bride makes the toast to the bride and bridegroom. If the bride's father has passed away or is absent, a relative or close family friend will toast instead. The bridegroom would then toast the bridesmaids. And then the best man would usually respond on behalf of the bridesmaids.

Nowadays, the bride may respond to a toast instead of her new husband. The chief bridesmaid may also decide to respond on behalf of the other bridesmaids, or indeed, if any one of the bridesmaids is a competent speaker, she may be elected to speak on their behalf. The mother of the bride may also be the one to toast the couple.

As you can see, these days just about anybody can make a wedding toast. At more formal weddings there may be:

- A Loyal Toast, if so desired, usually proposed by the MC.
- A toast to the bride and bridegroom by a brother or sister, or a close friend of either side of the family.
- A response by the bridegroom (he would also toast the bridesmaids at this time).
- A response by the best man.
- A toast to the bride's parents (the usual hosts for the wedding)

by a family friend or by the groom's parents.
- A response to this by the father of the bride, who might then propose a toast to his new in-laws—the parents of the groom.
- A response by the father of the groom.

No matter how many speeches are to be made, it is imperative that they are each kept to about three minutes. The MC should be ready to intervene if any one of the speakers embarks on a lengthy monologue. He should also warn speakers to be brief beforehand and remind them that any jokes included in their speech should be tasteful.

Sample Wedding Toast from the Father of the Bride

'I must admit, ladies and gentlemen, I had begun to think this day would never come. With four daughters and not one of them showing any sign of vacating the comfortable nest their mother has made for them, I'd given up hope. Therefore, I want to take this opportunity to welcome David into the nest—and I mean that, since they'll be living with us for the next two months before David takes up his post in London. This is a case of 'not losing a daughter, but gaining a son' if ever there were one!

'With my three other daughters here as bridesmaids today, I have to be careful not to say too many glowing things about Susan—certainly nothing that would indicate that she were any more talented, intelligent, witty and charming than any of my other girls. With a mother like Elizabeth, it comes as no surprise that Susan is the girl that she is—a girl who will make David an excellent companion in life … as long as they keep eating in restaurants. With 13 per cent in dressmaking at school and 11 per cent in her cooking classes, you can see she's a better dressmaker than a cook, but just between you and me, her dressmaking isn't that good either! Susan is a girl of many strengths—strengths that David has obviously seen or he wouldn't be here today. Both Elizabeth and I are very proud of Susan, and we know you join with us in wishing them both every happiness in the future.

'Elizabeth and I also want to take this opportunity to welcome David's parents, Josephine and Bruce, into our family. Fortunately, they're moving house and will be living near enough to drop in for a meal now and then. I believe they also have a couple of single sons so they'll be more than welcome.

'So, ladies and gentlemen, I ask you to charge your glasses and join with me in toasting the young couple, Susan and David, on this very happy occasion of their marriage.'

All of the guests, including the wedding party (but not Susan and David), will stand and say, 'To Susan and David'.

Sample Response from the Bridegroom

'Thank you Bill both for welcoming me into the McDougall family and also for warning me about Susan's sewing skills, or lack thereof. She warned me she wasn't much of a cook—and after eating a couple of her meals I found it was something of an understatement—but she didn't mention she couldn't sew. Still, since she speaks three languages, has two university degrees and has the sweetest, most generous nature of anyone I know, as you say, her strengths lie in other directions. I can assure you I'm enormously proud of her and I intend to be the best husband I can be, and a son-in-law you'll be proud of.

'Ladies and gentlemen, I'd like to thank Bill and

Elizabeth, not only for their efforts in making this day so memorable, but also for taking us in for the next two months until we go to London. And, difficult though it is to find the right words to thank my parents, I do thank them for all the years they've put up with my footy mates, my borrowing the car (and denting it), and my living at home for so long! The trouble is, when you have terrific 'mothers', like Elizabeth and my mum, Josephine, who wants to leave home?

'I may look as though I've "got it all together" today, but I can assure you that much of that is due to the efforts of my best man, Paul Sotherby, without whose ministrations I'd be a gibbering idiot. No one warned me that getting married was such a nerve-racking business, but Paul has been for me what I know Susan's sisters have been for her. Fiona, Skye and Briony, thank you for all you've done to help your sister over the past few weeks. I just hope we can be as supportive when your time comes! Finally, thank you to our flower girl and pageboy, who both did a fabulous job with the rings.

'So, could I ask you all to raise your glasses and drink to the three beautiful McDougall sisters ... the bridesmaids!'

Everyone will raise their glasses and echo, 'The bridesmaids'.

As I mentioned earlier, it is quite acceptable for one of the bridesmaids who enjoys speaking to make an acceptance speech on behalf of all of them. However, traditionally or if the bridesmaids prefer it, the speech or toast would come from the best man.

The best man should bear in mind the different ages and backgrounds of the guests and avoid tasteless jokes, which only he may enjoy. It's usual to be light-hearted at weddings, but use discretion at all costs!

Sample Response from the Best Man

'Ladies and gentlemen, David has done everything possible over the past few weeks to prevent me from speaking to you today. He tried to convince me that all the McDougall sisters wanted to speak on their own behalf—which no doubt they would do very competently—and that there would be absolutely no need for me to prepare anything (or to trouble myself). But, since David went to so much trouble to reveal most of my foibles and all of my misspent youth when he was best man at my wedding last year, I feel obliged to do the same here today.

'Today has been a beautiful day. I have never seen Susan look so lovely, and I must say that David looks ten years younger without his beard. (Turning to look at bride and bridegroom) You make a handsome couple and I wish you both all the best for the future. (Looking back at guests) Elizabeth and Bill have excelled themselves, not only in producing four lovely daughters, but also in arranging this wonderful reception today. Now, before I tell you all about the bridegroom, (looking at bridegroom) let me take this opportunity of thanking you, David, for your complimentary words to the bridesmaids. They thank you for the pearls you gave them earlier today, and incidentally, they're very interested in accepting your kind offer to help with their wedding arrangements when "their time comes"." (Looking back to guests)

If you're an accomplished speaker, then you may care to regale the guests with one or two (no more) amusing incidents concerning David's past or perhaps something amusing to do with your role as best man in the lead-up to the wedding. This will depend on your proficiency in giving speeches and on the bridegroom's desire for you to do so. In any case, your speech should end with a toast to the bride and bridegroom.

'I ask you to join me, ladies and gentlemen, (looking at bride and groom) in toasting our beautiful bride, Susan, and her husband, David. To Susan and David.'

As before, the guests will simply repeat, 'To Susan and David'.

The best man should read all the congratulatory messages at this time; he should, however, have pre-read them so that he can censor them. Sexual innuendo and bawdy jokes are tasteless and out of place and are best kept for the buck's night.

REFERENCES

1. Bentley, BA, 1972, *English for the Higher School Certificate*, Hogbin, Poole (Printers) Pty Ltd, Sydney.

2. Bowden, J, 2000, *Making the Father of the Bride's Speech*, How to Books Ltd, Oxford.

3. Carnegie, D, 1997, *How to Develop Self-confidence and Influence People by Public Speaking*, Random House, London.

4. Cooney, B, 2002, *Talk Sense! A commonsense approach to speaking in a group*, Michelle Anderson Publishing Pty Ltd, Melbourne.

5. Davidson, J, 2003, *The Complete Guide to Public Speaking*, Wiley & Sons, New Jersey.

6. Dean, JJ, 1992, *Effective Speaking: Here's how*, Boolarong Publications, Brisbane.

7. Herman, J & D, 1998, *Toasts For All Occasions*, Career Press, New Jersey.

8. Irvin, D, 2000, *The Everything Toasts Book*, Adams Media Corporation, Holbrook.

9. Lamerton, J, 2001, *Everything You Need to Know About Public Speaking*, HarperCollins, Glasgow.

10. Leeds, D, 1988, *Powerspeak: The complete guide to public speaking and presentation*, Judy Piatkus (Publishers) Ltd, London.

11. McCarthy, P, & Hatcher, C, 1996, *Speaking Persuasively: The essential guide to giving dynamic presentations and speeches*, Allen & Unwin, Sydney.

12. Rathus, ER, & Morelle, RL, 1987, *Speaking in Public*, The Jacaranda Press, Milton.

13. Rowe, P, 2004, *Business Etiquette: Achieving a competitive edge in business*, New Holland Publishers (Australia) Pty Ltd, Sydney.

14. Rowe, P, 2000, *Manners for the Millennium: Etiquette for men and women*, Oxenford Press, Sanctuary Cove.

What do people say about me?

'Patsy made a great job of energising and encouraging our sales-people. She's super-enthusiastic and heaps of fun.'
Sylvia Bradshaw, General Manger, Leader Newspapers

'Patsy Rowe—a livewire with a natural flair for communicating with humour—is one of the most passionate, energetic and inter-esting speakers I have used for both in-house staff as well as VIP client seminars. She lights up the room with her charm and enthusiasm for life.'
Jillian Talbot, Westpac Business Development Manager

'Patsy Rowe is well known to the Institute as we sell her books and invite her to speak to our client base. As one of its suite of events programs AIM offers Business Etiquette seminars. We chose Patsy to run these seminars because she is an effective communicator who puts a lot of effort into ensuring her presentations are both informative and entertaining.'
Cath Healy, Australian Institute of Management, Manager, Meeting and Events

'The excellent feedback from last night's presentation has been overwhelming with everyone who attended feeling that the session was perfectly targeted. Many people, I think, were surprised to be so entertained.'
Paula Knudsen, Senior State Development Officer, Department of State Development

For more information visit www.etiquette.com.au

BOOKS BY PATSY ROWE

The Little Book of Etiquette

Business Etiquette…achieving a competitive edge in business

Manners For the Millennium…etiquette for men & women

Secret Women's Business…how to get it all & keep it

You Are Leaving Tuesday Aren't You?

Am I Having Fun Yet?

No Sweat, Not to Worry, She'll be Jake

Secret Women's Business Journal
List your lovers or your laundry—whichever you have the most of! This beautifully bound, hardcover notebook is a great gift idea for any occasion.

Secret Women's Business Inspiration Cards
All 52 cards—one for each week of the year—offer useful advice for achieving a balanced life in this fast-paced modern world.